A RHAPSODY FOR JOSEPH,

The Quintessential Father

A RHAPSODY FOR JOSEPH,

The Quintessential Father

JACOB C. TONY,
MD, MRCP (UK), MRCPI

Xulon Press

Xulon Press
2301 Lucien Way #415
Maitland, FL 32751
407.339.4217
www.xulonpress.com

Unless otherwise indicated, Scripture quotations taken from The
New Revised Standard Version, Catholic Edition For India, Published
by Thomas Nelson, Theological Publications In India, Bangalore,
Copyright © 1993. Used by permission. All rights reserved.

Printed in the United States of America.

Paperback SBN-13: 978-1-6628-1405-1
Ebook ISBN-13: 978-1-6628-1406-8

DEDICATION

I entrust my son Kevin to St. Joseph. Father Joseph, you are the father and patron of the mystical body of Christ, and therefore Kevin is your son too.

ACKNOWLEDGMENT

I am grateful to Kavitha Susan Jacob, MD for proofreading the manuscript. I thank Erica Coulter and all the nice people at Xulon Press who made this project a success.

TABLE OF CONTENTS

JOSEPH AND THE POWER OF THE UNSAID

Joseph does not speak a single word in the Bible, yet he was the only man among all the children of Adam to have the unique privilege of becoming the foster father of Jesus and the chaste spouse of Virgin Mary. He is an enigma wrapped in a mystery, and for that reason I am a bit nervous to write about him. How do you write about a man who does not speak? Then it dawned upon me that there is meaning in silence. It is said that actions speak louder than words, and this aphorism is very true in the life of St. Joseph.

We must study Joseph by not what he said, but by observing the tremendous power of the unsaid in his life. There is more meaning in the unsaid, in personal communications. Diplomats, poets, men of letters, and painters convey ideas and meanings through their meaningful silence. Silence is a powerful language when it is accompanied by fruitful actions. So, we see that Joseph is speaking without talking.

What does he talk? He obeys God and tells us to obey God. He remains chaste and teaches us about the beauty of chastity in a world infested with impurity. He is a strong father to Jesus, and thereby instructs men to "man up" as fathers. He is loyal to His wife, Mary, and thereby shows men the virtue of fidelity in marriage. He works hard and demonstrates the dignity of labor. He was the pillar of his family, and thereby showed us the three-fold function of man as "the prophet, priest, and king" of his family.

St Joseph is speaking abundantly through his life, and I am determined to listen to him. This is going to be an adventurous journey with Joseph, and I am looking forward to it.

THE HOLY FAMILY

"Your wife will be like a fruitful vine within your house; your children will be like olive shoots around your table." – God designed each family to be like this. However, we have corrupted it by redefining sex, biology, reproduction, and even the concept of family! Future generations will see the disruption of the social fabric and total mayhem when they start "engineering" the very fundamental blocks of human civilization.

God has set humans apart and in fact placed us on a high rock. We are created in the image of God. He created man and woman and gave them children. God is glorified in a family where the wife is a fruitful vine and her children are like olive shoots. When traditional roles, morality, and sacrificial giving are threatened, then families will invariably start dissipating.

Joseph, Mary, and Jesus are our model. Holy Family is the compass that guides our small families to its safe harbor.

THE FIRST EUCHARISTIC PROCESSION OVER THE HILLS OF JUDEA

The gospel of Luke describes the first Eucharistic procession. When Mary realized that she conceived the unborn God Incarnate in her womb, she got up in a hurry to share his presence to the world. That moment, Mary became the tabernacle of the Most High. In fact, she became the Ark of the Covenant. Mary undertook the dangerous journey over the hill country to see Elizabeth. It must have been a 100-mile trip from Nazareth to the house of Zechariah, and the road was deceptively dangerous and infested with bandits. There is reason to believe that Joseph ,who was betrothed to Mary, accompanied her on this dangerous journey. Joseph was the priest of the house, and he accompanied Mary, the tabernacle, who held the body of God Incarnate in her womb. It therefore was a Eucharistic procession. In Judeo-Christian thought, the husband is the priest of the house, and therefore it was apt for Joseph to accompany Mary to the house of Zechariah.

FIFTY-THOUSAND YEARS, 108 BILLION HOMO SAPIENS, AND ONE ST. JOSEPH

Modern Homo sapiens first walked the earth about 50,000 years ago. The Population Reference Bureau based in Washington DC estimates that about 108 billion people have existed in this world since then. Why did God choose St. Joseph from among the 108 billion people to become the foster father of Jesus? What made this man unique? He must have been adorned with many physical, mental, and spiritual gifts or else God would not have allowed His Son, Jesus, to become the foster son of Joseph. There is something hidden in Joseph that ordinary men cannot see. It is prudential and profitable to study the life of St. Joseph. We all can learn from him. It is difficult for a modern man to comprehend the mind of Joseph as we are detached from simple obedience and uncorrupted love. St. Joseph gives us an opportunity to re-learn our lost innocence.

A TYPOLOGY OF CONFIRMATION

When Virgin Mary enters the house of Zechariah and Elizabeth, a miracle of unprecedented proportion occurs. Mary greets Elizabeth; and that is all she does. See the cascading effect of a simple greeting. Mary is bearing God, and therefore her greetings are weighty. The moment Mary greeted Elizabeth, the Holy Spirit came upon Elizabeth, and she started prophesying. In addition, John the Baptist who was still in the womb of his mother, Elizabeth, leaped in the womb. Elizabeth cried out "Blessed are you among women and blessed is the fruit of your womb. And why has this happened to me, that the mother of my Lord comes to me?" Zechariah, the husband of Elizabeth, was a priest who ministered at the altar of incense in the Temple of Jerusalem. It put him in the position of a high priest, and the Holy Spirit came upon his wife and unborn son under his

4

watchful eyes. It looks as if it was a typology of Christian confirmation. I remember my own first holy communion and confirmation. I received the first holy communion from our parish priest, but was confirmed by the Bishop of Kottayam, India. The bishop (high priest), imparts the sacrament of confirmation. Mary is the mother of God, but the confirmation still occurs in the presence of Zechariah, the high priest. I see parallels between this incident and the sacrament of confirmation.

JOSEPH, THE SON OF DAVID

Joseph was the son of David, and therefore by lineage Jesus Himself became the Son of David through Joseph. He was instrumental in conferring the title "Son of David" to Jesus, because he was the foster father of Jesus. Joseph was born into the royal family of David, though he became a poor carpenter at a later stage in his life. He behaved with royal dignity, even when he knew that his wife, Mary, was pregnant before marriage. He was a just man, a humble man, and above all a man of purity. He should be the model for every man, because God in all eternity selected Joseph to be the "Man of His house." Mary submitted to him and Jesus obeyed him unconditionally. Tell me, besides Virgin Mary; is there anyone greater than Joseph among the created human beings? Tell me the name of a patriarch, prophet, apostle, or saint greater than Joseph? Joseph therefore has a dignity greater than all the saints (except Virgin Mary who is the mother of God.)

Dear Father Joseph, I entrust my family under your mantle. Watch over them and defend them from the darts of the malicious enemy.

JOSEPH ESCAPED THE SWORD OF HEROD, BUT ZECHARIAH DID NOT

Herod, the Great, was an insecure man infested with jealousy. He wanted to hold on to power by any means. In the process, he shed much blood. The Bible talks about him getting jealous about the newborn king. In his attempt to eliminate any claim on his throne, he ordered the killing of infants below the age of two. The angel warned Joseph in a dream, and therefore his life was spared. However, Zechariah was not lucky. The gospel of Matthew mentions about Zechariah being killed between the temple and the altar, and many church fathers believe that it was Zechariah, the father of John the Baptist.

Zechariah shed his blood while trying to protect infant John. St Joseph escaped the sword of Herod. However, years later Herod Antipas beheaded John the Baptist for preaching against adultery and incest. Speaking truth to power is costly then and now. It has not changed.

WHERE WAS ADAM WHEN THE SERPENT WAS FLIRTING WITH HIS WIFE?

This is not a question to Adam, but a question to every man. The postmodern society is witnessing a tremendous erosion of manhood at an accelerating pace. Manhood is undergoing decimation by a thousand cuts. External and internal forces are at work to destroy true manhood, authentic womanhood, and innocent childhood. Men, Women, and children are facing identity crisis of unprecedented proportion. It all started with the spiritual battle in the garden between man, woman, and the serpent. However, modern times have speeded up this battle to dizzying heights. Where was Adam when the serpent was talking to his wife? Some theologians believe that Adam was there, right in the middle of that exchange between the woman and the snake. He passively stepped aside when the snake freely tempted his wife. He did not prevent the conversation, and he refused to stand up for his right. He regressed into his shell rather than actively fighting against the serpent.

Today, men are regressing even more than before. Chivalry, honor, character, and integrity has disappeared from the modern lexicon. Spineless, shapeless, and infantile men are spending too much time before televisions and computers, that they have no time for internal formation. They are facing massive identity crisis. Lack of male role models have led families into irremediable despair. Wives have lost faith in husbands and children are wandering around without direction. Meanwhile politicians, social engineers, self-serving technocrats, philosophers of death, perverted celebrities and soulless billionaires are creeping into the most intimate and private spaces of our sacred family lives through the medium of propaganda television and social media. What are men doing? Like Adam, they are regressing into the basement to watch soap operas to avoid responsibility.

The iconoclasts have destroyed true icons of manhood like St. Joseph and raised dubious and perverse idols of "manhood" in our own homes.

JESUS OF NAZARETH, SON OF DAVID, AND THE BLIND MAN OF JERICHO

In the gospel of Luke, Jesus is seen approaching Jericho. A blind beggar was sitting by the roadside. When he heard the crowd passing by, he asked what was happening. They told him "Jesus of Nazareth is passing by." Then he shouted, "Jesus, Son of David, have mercy on me." Jesus asked him, "What do you want me to do for you?" He replied, "Lord, let me see again." Jesus commanded, "Receive your sight." The bible records that he immediately regained sight.

In this incident, I see two revelations. How did people address Jesus? They called him Jesus of Nazareth. Why did they call him so? It was simply because his father Joseph decided to build their house in Nazareth. The second revelation is messianic in nature. The beggar calls Jesus "The Son of David." Jesus is descended from the line of King David through his foster father Joseph. Again, Jesus inherited this title because of Joseph.

Some fanatics in their extreme view try to isolate Jesus from his father Joseph and Mother Mary. It is a folly to do so. Jesus is not detached from his parents or people. He is still called the Son of David and Jesus of Nazareth, thanks to Joseph.

8

JOSEPH, THE CUSTODIAN OF THE HUMANITY OF JESUS

Jesus is true God and true man. He is the Son of God. The Gospel of John is about the Son of God. John begins the gospel like this, "In the beginning was the Word, and the Word was with God, and the Word was God. He was in the beginning with God." However, Matthew writes about the human nature of Jesus when he starts the gospel like this, "An account of the genealogy of Jesus the Messiah, the son of David, the son of Abraham." Matthew was highlighting Jesus as the Son of Man, while John was interested in projecting Jesus as the Son of God. Jesus had both natures, and therefore he was the Son of God and the Son of Man at the same time. The humanity of Jesus went through all the phases of a human being: he was an embryo, a fetus, a newborn baby, a toddler, a child, a teenager and a youth. By living through these phases of human life he sanctified human existence in all its forms. Joseph was the custodian of Jesus through all these human phases. He protected him, sheltered him, fed him, and even clothed him. Joseph was intimately associated with the humanity of Jesus.

A LONELY MONK WALKING IN THE RAIN UNDER A LEAKING UMBRELLA

Sometime in the late 1980s, I read an article about the notorious Chinese Communist dictator Mao Tse-Tung in an Indian newspaper. One of his quotes caught my attention. Apparently, Mao told the famous American Journalist Edgar

Snow that he was a lonely monk walking in the rain under a leaking umbrella. The quote evokes the powerful imagery of a solitary man walking the face of the earth battling the elements of nature with minimal tools at his disposal. Mao is known to lie, and deception was one of his strategies. It is obvious that he was playing to the minds of his Western admirers. However, the imagery is beautiful, and I often use this metaphor when I describe the faith-walk of a Christian. When God calls, we must leave everything behind and step into the unknown. Once we have stepped into the unknown, what follows is a journey through unchartered territories. It is a scary and adventurous journey. There is a constant sense of insecurity and a sense of dread and darkness which saints call "The dark night of the soul." It is a constant battle against doubt, despair, and despondency in the backdrop of this elusive feeling called "faith." We must walk by faith (faith is defined as our hope in the unseen), and since faith is not a palpable material reality but an unseen transcendental assurance, the walk with God can be a huge challenge. I have borrowed this imagery from a communist dictator to best describe my own faith walk through three continents. It was sometime during this difficult pilgrimage that I realized that St. Joseph himself was a man who walked in the rain under a leaking umbrella. Life was not easy for St. Joseph, and though he was the father of Jesus, he was not called to live in a palace but rather in the wastelands of Nazareth and Egypt.

When I started writing about St. Joseph, I wondered what is there to write about him, but halfway through the writing, I realized that I cannot stop writing about him!

JOSEPH IN EGYPT

We all know the story of Joseph, the patriarch, and his life in Egypt. It is well recorded in the bible. However, the life of Joseph, the carpenter, is practically unknown. We know that he went to Egypt along with his wife Mary and Son, Jesus, but we do not have any details about their stay in Egypt.

Did Joseph, the Carpenter, meet a "Potiphar" in his life too? Was he tempted by Egyptian seductresses like the way Joseph, the patriarch was tempted? Did he face allegations against his integrity? Did he see the Pharaoh? We do not know the answer to any of these questions, but we know one thing: Joseph was a chaste spouse to Mary all throughout his life! Mary was born without the original sin, but Joseph, on the other hand, was born with original sin like you and me! Mary, being immaculately conceived, had no inherent propensity to commit sins, but Joseph was different. He was not immaculately conceived, and since he was born with the original sin, he had to fight against his own fallen nature. This makes Joseph a true hero. This makes Josephs a true warrior from the tribe of David. This alone adds great luster to the life of Joseph, the peasant! In spite of his fallen nature, Joseph remained just, humble, and chaste!

He was indeed a great man. He was truly a man's man.

THE PLUMB LINE OF JOSEPH

Joseph, the son of David, was a carpenter. He was a builder by occupation. He must have built many houses, and surely, he would have used the tools of his trade to build houses. A plumb line was an inevitable tool in the hands of a builder. Ancient Egyptians used plumb lines to build the great pyramids. Joseph must have used plumb lines too to build houses in Egypt and Nazareth. He must have taught his Son Jesus to use plumb lines. Interestingly, God, the Son, had revealed the images of plumb lines to many prophets of old. He showed a plumb line to prophet Amos. Prophet Amos wrote, "Thus He showed me: and, behold, the Lord stood upon a wall made by a plumb line, with a plumb line in His hand. And the Lord said unto me, Amos, what do you see? And I said a plumb line. Then said the Lord, Behold, I will set a plumb line in the midst of my people Israel: I will not again pass by them anymore." Amos understood the meaning of the vision. A plumb line is used in construction, and it is used further to test a building when it is built. Plumb lines are used to see if the wall is vertical and upright. The integrity of the wall is tested against the standards set by the plumb line. If a building is built without a plumb line, it will not last the test of time. It will eventually collapse. The great pyramids, domes and cathedrals of the world were built against the standards set by plumb lines, and therefore they stood the test of time.

God is the builder, and we are his temples. He sets a plumb line before us. If our walls are not upright, he will break and reconstruct it until we align to His standards. His plumb lines are His commandments. His plumb lines are the beatitudes of Christ. His plumb lines are the highest moral standards. We need to see His standards, commandments, and precepts every minute of our life or else we might lose our path to heaven.

Jesus, the Son of Joseph, is the master carpenter. His plumb line is before me. I hope and pray that I can live by His standards.

JOSEPH, THE OBEDIENT SON

Joseph, the Patriarch, was a very obedient son. When Jacob told him to go the fields in search of his brothers, he obeyed his father without any reservations. The obedience of Joseph cost him much: he had to face Egyptian captivity, simply because he obeyed his father. The rest is history.

Years later, Joseph, the foster father of Jesus, was told to go on exile to Egypt. The Heavenly Father sent His messenger to Joseph and instructed him to leave Israel. Joseph obeyed God unconditionally. Joseph had to take his teenage wife and Baby Jesus to an unknown pagan nation with strange language, customs, and beliefs. It was not an easy task.

Joseph is the model of obedience. We can learn a lot from him.

THE FOSTER FATHER OF TRUTH

What is truth? Truth, in its essence, is immutable. It cannot change with the fashion of the day. It is an objective, outside reality, that cannot change with the whims and fancies of men. It can never be interpreted with the subjective flavor of the rich and the powerful. Truth calls us to sacrifice the pleasures and gains of life, solely for the sake of knowing truth. The reward of truth is unadulterated truth and nothing else. Truth does not offer fringe benefits of any kind. Truth is solid, like granite, while the passion of men is flimsy, like fluid. The man who searches the truth will abandon career, fame, and fortune solely for the sake of truth, while the prophets of falsehood will betray truth for thirty pieces of silver. The man of truth is hated by the world because the children of falsehood want to distort truth and sell truth for their own financial or career benefits. For Christians truth is not an epistemological question, but an actual person. Truth has a name and his name is Jesus Christ. Jesus tells us that he is the Truth. Truth is the Second Person of the Holy Trinity. People who hate the rigors of truth find alternate spirituality in mindfulness, yogic posturing, and tantric healing. They go for psychedelic therapy in Amazonian rainforests and gulp the psychedelic brew called ayahuasca under the watchful eyes of shamans for spiritual healing. Truth liberates us from self-love while falsehood drives us to narcissism, elitism, pride, and lust.

Jesus Christ is the Truth. St. Joseph guarded the Infant Truth like a warrior. He is therefore the foster father of Truth.

RUN, JOSEPH, RUN!

Run, Joseph. Run away. Do not stay for a minute. Run for your life. Wake up! Put your wife and son on the donkey. Leave before the daybreak.

Poor Joseph, his life was nothing but running from pillar to post! If you stay in the city, Herod will kill your wife and child. Do not waste a minute. Save your family. Pack your bags and flee from the sinful city!

In the Old Testament we see another Joseph. He was running all the time. First, he was taken away from the city where his brothers lived. He thought Potiphar would give him security. But Potiphar's wife wanted to sleep with Joseph. So, Joseph ran for his life and in the process, he even left his cloak behind.

Lot was told to flee from the city of Sodom. He fled in a hurry with his family. The city was so bad that he was instructed not even to look back. Noah was asked to flee from evildoers. He was asked to build an Ark to save his family.

Flee from sinful afflictions. Run for your life. Save your wife. Save your children!

EXTRA FURNITURE AND A NEW ROBE FOR JESUS

Joseph is in his shop. He is building ploughs and furniture. If he builds extra furniture, he could buy a new robe for Baby Jesus or replace Mary's old robe with a new one! Joseph is working hard!

Joseph clothed the emperor of the universe. Joseph fed the God of the Universe. This is nothing but a miracle. This is what I call "Poetry in motion." What a beautiful concept; the man works in the field; the woman tends the children and the children obey their parents. We have "Social engineered" ourselves from the concept of holy family and have alienated ourselves from "family life." Instead we have created "engineered marriages" and "synthetic trash." What we do today in the West is an abomination in the eyes of God; and, if it is not an abomination to God, then God Himself has to re-write the bible for "modern man" and "modern families."

THE POOR DESCENDANT OF KING DAVID

Joseph lived in a time in history known for its brutality. Romans occupied Palestine and enthroned a psychopathic person as the puppet king of Israel. King Herod was paranoid and sociopathic by nature and he even massacred his own family members without remorse. In addition, he taxed the people of Palestine to build fortresses and temples. The common men in Palestine lived under the double yoke of Herod and Augustus with great fear and suspicion. Joseph was a descendant of David, but he kept a very low profile. The descendants of King David were poor peasants, and no one even mentioned the name of David for fear of retribution from Herod and Augustus. Neither Herod nor Augustus wanted to hear the name of King David because they thought that the descendants of David would be a threat to their thrones. It was in this background that the Wise Men from the East came to Herod's palace looking for the newborn king. No wonder, Herod, the madman of Palestine, ordered the massacre of the innocents!

The descendants of the aristocrats are always a threat to the sensual and vicious people in power. However, God works in mysterious ways through the poor descendants of the aristocrats. He brought the "King of Kings" out of the house Joseph, the son of David. Joseph might have been poor, but he was of royal lineage. His ancestry can be traced all the way back to king David!

THE ANGEL OF JOSEPH

We see in the bible that angels frequently communicated with Joseph. They revealed secrets and even warned Joseph about impending dangers. Have the angels stopped working in the twenty-first century? No way, the angels are still alive and kicking!

The church teaches that an angel is assigned to each one of us. We do not see them, but they are protecting us from hidden dangers. The voice of the guardian angel is the voice of our conscience. It is a soft voice of righteousness urging us to take the path of righteousness. We are drowning the soft voice of the Guardian Angel amongst the sounds and furies of this madding crowd. Therefore, we are not aware of the existence of Guardian Angels.

Joseph constantly listened to his interior voice, and therefore learned to conduct his life in the most upright way. We have much to learn from Joseph!

DECISIONS AND CONSEQUENCES

Joseph made a decision: a decision that no other man has ever made. He, therefore, had a unique lifestyle without precedents. He had no role models. He was alone. To be a "solitary monk" is a tough decision. He had no other "monks" to imitate or even discuss life-issues. He had to craft his own life-path. He had to steer his own ship. When he became tired, he conversed with God. When he was thrown into the tough realities of life, he bore the yoke of life like a beast of burden. He did not complain because he knew that complaining was counterproductive. He worked, prayed, and hoped for the best, and that was all he could do. He was a peasant with a purpose, and his purpose in life was even unknown to him. Life was a day to day struggle for existence, but even in the midst of these mundane tasks he found God. That alone makes Joseph a true hero!

Tradition says that Joseph took a vow of chastity before God. Well, it was a contract that Joseph "Signed" with God. No one forced him to do that. He took that vow out of freewill. Then, what is the point in complaining? Joseph was not exempted from the original sin unlike his spouse Mary. Joseph therefore was like each one of us, even in the fact that he was born with the original sin. Mary was born without original sin (immaculately conceived), and hence to guard her virginity before, during, and after the birth of Christ would have been easy for her. Joseph however kept his vow of chastity, even though he was born with the original sin. In other words, the struggle to remain chaste would have been bigger for Joseph than Mary. In my eyes, this makes Joseph a bigger hero!

Joseph had only one path to follow: the path of total surrender, and obedience. Any other path would have led him to disaster. Joseph, however, honored his word and lived by his word. That alone makes Joseph an honorable man.

FROM JOSEPH TO JOSEPH

This is my story unfolding, as I walk from one Joseph to another Joseph. It took twelve years and lot of pain before I realized the story of a poor Joseph. I came to know the first Joseph in 1995. I realized the story of the second Joseph in 2007. Years have passed and God in his wisdom revealed to me the great story of a beautiful creation of God: the story of Joseph.

I acquainted the first Joseph through my evangelical, protestant, and charismatic Catholic friends. The first Joseph was deceived by his brothers. He was thrown to a pit. He was sold as a slave. He was accused falsely and imprisoned in an Egyptian prison. He saw dreams and visions. He became the second highest authority figure in ancient Egypt. God brought his brothers and father to him. They apologized to Joseph. Joseph forgave them. This is a true story. The story is similar to the story of Lincoln, the story of rags to riches, the walk from the log house to the white house. This story inspired me to accomplish my dreams. This story motivated me to go forward in Christianity. I went to churches and sang and clapped with others to celebrate the gift of God. I still love it. Geographically, I was in England when this happened.

In 2003, we left England and moved to America. My training and job demanded all my time. The dream of the Joseph of Egypt looked distant to me. It was at this time that I identified the Joseph of Nazareth.

Joseph of Nazareth was probably uneducated. He was a manual laborer. He was a poor peasant. His story is a forgotten story. He never made it to the court of Herod or to the court of Caesar. He married a woman and found out that she was already pregnant with the Child of God. He observed celibacy. He had to take his pregnant wife to Bethlehem, where he was rejected by everyone. He could only provide a manger for Mary. He had to run to Egypt with Mary and the Son of God to protect them from harm. Interestingly he never asked, "Why do you put me through this? What have I done? Isn't Jesus your own son? Why can't you provide Mary with a decent place to deliver her son? Can't you protect even the son of God from the wrath of a mortal man?" We see that he was just an "obedient fool". I still love this "obedient fool". I acquainted this Joseph through old rosary bearing Catholics.

It is in the school of "obedient fools" that saints are trained. It is in the school of poverty, obedience, and chastity, that great church fathers are created. It is in the pain of the daily monotonous routine that God teaches his deepest lessons. It is in the manger that we see Jesus. It is in the flight to Egypt that we realize our vulnerability and God's magnanimity. It is in our daily chores that God strips our spiritual pride and clothes us with humility. The story of Joseph's life may not make a Hollywood story; however, the aroma of his story will excel the aroma of the lilies and roses of Sharon.

THE TEMPLE OF SOLOMON

Solomon built a beautiful temple. He then prayed, "When your people go to war against their enemies, wherever you send them, and when they pray to you towards this city you have chosen and the temple I have built for your Name, then hear from heaven their prayer and their plea, and uphold their cause." Unfortunately, Solomon's temple doesn't exist anymore!

Joseph, the foster father of Jesus, was a direct descendant of King Solomon. Jesus said, "Destroy this Temple, and I will raise it again in three days." Jesus was referring to himself when he made the above statement. Therefore, we are supposed to pray to Jesus, the true Temple, before we go to war against our enemies. Who are our enemies? Our enemies are our evil temptations. We must pray to Jesus to fight our battles against the evil one.

Jesus is the true descendant of David, and he is in fact the temple of Solomon. Jesus has this claim to Davidic Dynasty because of Joseph, the foster father of Jesus!

WHEN DAVID PRAYED FOR JOSEPH—

Long ago, King David went before the Lord of Israel and prayed for St Joseph! He prayed, "Who am I, O Lord God, and what is my family, that you have brought me this far? And as if this were not enough in your sight, O God, you have spoken about the future of the **house of your servant**." David said this in response to God's promise that He would raise up one of David's offspring as a king forever. Clearly, God was promising that He would bring forth Jesus, the Messiah, from the house of David. This was made possible because Joseph, the foster father of Jesus, was a direct descendant of King David. King David foresaw the promise and prayed

21

for his descendants. Many of David's descendants, Solomon included, were rebels who worshipped pagan gods and goddesses. Joseph was an exception to that rule. Joseph was a just man, and therefore God honored him by making him the foster father of Jesus. The fruit of the prayers of David for his descendants fell upon St. Joseph. He inherited the promise to become the "Father of the Messiah."

Joseph was the true descendant of David in flesh, blood, and spirit!

A JOSEPH IS NEEDED TO SAVE MARY FROM PUBLIC DISGRACE!

Mary is the Mother of God. She conceived the Second Person of the Trinity. What was conceived in her was from the Holy Spirit, the Third Person of the Trinity. She was the daughter of God the Father: The First Person of the Trinity. Still, when she became pregnant while betrothed to Joseph; she was exposed to the risk of public disgrace. She risked shame and even death. As per the Law of Moses, a woman found pregnant before marriage could be stoned to death!

Who on earth could save Mary from disgrace? Her mother Ann could not save her. Her father Joachim could not save her. Ironically, even Jesus could not save her from humiliation. Interestingly, even the Holy Trinity needed help! God needed the help of a man. Only one man could save Mary from humiliation. Only one man could save Mary from disgrace. Only one man could save Mary from the stone-throwers of Israel. Only one man could save Mary from the public fury. Only one man could save her from the law of Moses. His name was Joseph.

Joseph was not an emperor. Joseph was not a priest. He was a day laborer. He was a carpenter. He was planning to divorce Mary quietly. Joseph's mind must be changed. So God interfered. He sent his beloved angel to Joseph. Joseph accepted Mary.

There are situations in life where men are needed to fix divine problems! God works through people. Joseph was the only being, from all created beings, that had the capability to save Mary from the shame. Joseph stepped in and Mary was saved. Nobody would ever laugh at Mary. Nobody would ever belittle Mary. No one would dare to approach Mary with unholy intentions. In fact, Joseph turned the equation around. He accepted Mary and then Mary said, "Generations to come will call me Blessed". Elizabeth prophesied "Blessed are you. Blessed is the fruit of your womb". Joseph's single act of obedience turned a potential problem into a potent source of grace. Mary became the Mother of God. Mary became the wife of Joseph. Mary became the bearer of God (Theotokos).

Joseph never uttered a word in the bible. He was not a man of words. He was a man of mighty deeds. Father Joseph, save us from disgrace and shame.

FROM APE TO ANGEL-A CALL TO HOLINESS

The interesting dichotomy of human existence is that we are striving to develop the heart of an angel, while trapped in the framework of an ape! Evolutionary biology teaches us that humans and apes had a common ancestor. The nature of the ape is still within us! We have hunger and so we eat. Sometimes to get steady supply of food and resources we fight with each other. We have reproductive organs and so we procreate. We crave for sex and even fight to win partners. However, angels do not have to worry about food or sex! Still the bible is asking us to develop the higher nature of angels while trapped in the physical body of mortal humans. In other words, we are called to become holy.

My lesser nature pulls me down. I look for role models. There are Catholic mystics and monks who became saints. Most of them were unmarried people who lived in convents or monasteries. How can I imitate them? I am a married man living in twenty-first century America. I am not a mystic or a monk and I dare not become one. Then I discovered a married peasant named Joseph. He was a regular guy who had a mundane lifestyle. However, he was a just man. He could live under the same roof as Jesus.

Joseph, the just man, is my model. I could evolve from an ape to an angel by imitating Joseph!

JOSEPH NAMED HIM JESUS!

The name above all the names is the name of Jesus. At the mention of the name of Jesus, everything in heaven and earth kneel before Him. Interestingly, it was a humble carpenter named Joseph who was given the privilege to name the Son of God with the name Jesus! It was the right of Joseph to name his foster Son with the name Jesus!

Joseph is unique among all the men who walked on the face of earth. There was no man like Joseph before him and there will never be a man like Joseph in the future!

JOSEPH, THE HOLY FOOL

Joseph, unfortunately, is a forgotten man. Mary is honored, for the right reasons. She even receives "Hyperdulia." But who is Joseph?

Joseph was a laborer who labored without honor and died before seeing the fruits of his labor. Mary saw the fruits of her labor. She initiated the miracle at Cana, heard the teachings of Jesus, and saw him healing the sick. She saw His sacrifice at Calvary, resurrection from the dead, and ascension to heaven! She received the Holy Spirit in the Upper Room and saw Peter, the first Pope. She even became the mother of the early Christians. Poor Joseph had no such honors. He was a "Nobody" in the annals of the early church.

Joseph never said a word in the bible. He was a peasant who fed God and His mother. He died in obscurity. He is a forgotten man!

THE CELESTIAL TRINITY AND "THE TERRESTRIAL TRINITY"

The hall mark of authentic Christianity is our belief in the Trinity. We believe in the Father who is the maker of all things, the Son, the redeemer, and the Holy Spirit who is our advocate. Jesus the son of God became the Son of man in the fullness of time. God the Father entrusted him to Joseph and Mary while he was on earth. The Son of God is part of the celestial trinity with the Father and the Holy Spirit. Jesus, the son of man is part of the "terrestrial trinity" with Joseph and Mary. Jesus, the Son of God, is inseparable from Jesus, the son of man. He is truly the son of God and the son of man. Jesus shared his terrestrial life intimately with Mary and Joseph. Jesus called Mary "Mom" and Joseph "Dad". Jesus the son of man was, is and will be the son of Joseph and Mary too. This is the greatest honor for human race-God became man and lived among us. He lived in a human womb. He was nursed by a woman. He was fed and clothed by a man. He was carried in the arms of a man and a woman.

Jesus himself has said that God is the God of Abraham, Isaac, and Jacob. He is the God of the living and not the God of the dead. Jesus is therefore the son of Joseph and Mary not only in time but also in eternity. Through Mary, Jesus the son of God became Jesus the son of man. He made himself a part of the "terrestrial trinity" and therefore became Emmanuel (God is with us).

How can we honor the Son without honoring his parents? If God, the creator, honored Joseph and Mary as the parents of his Son how can we deny honor to Joseph and Mary? Stop intellectualizing and learn from babes. Honor Joseph and Mary: you will only honor their Son more by honoring them. I believe we are not honoring Joseph and Mary enough. We are not thanking them enough. In fact, many of us are hurting Jesus by thrusting swords into the heart of Mary by denying her perpetual virginity, Immaculate Conception, and her unique position in human history as the Mother of God (Theotokos). Stop insulting Mary, the Ark of the Covenant. In the Old Testament the high priest had to consecrate himself and wait for one year before he could enter the Holy of Holies and prostrate before the Ark of the Covenant. In the Old Testament God spoke to people from the mercy seat on the Ark of the Covenant. Nobody could touch the Ark of the Covenant, but the Levites had to carry it on their shoulders on poles.

Do you think anybody can defile Mary, the living Ark of the Covenant? Do you think God has stopped speaking from his Mercy seat on the living Ark of the Covenant (Mary)? You will never call Mary blessed unless you are filled with the Holy Spirit. Elizabeth was filled with the Holy Spirit at the mere arrival of Mary and called her the Mother of Adonai (Mother of my Lord). If you deny the respect due to Mary it only means that you are not filled with the Holy Spirit. You may speak in tongues, you may prophecy, but you will miss your point if you miss Mary.

JOSEPH AND JONAS

Jonas had a job to do but he abdicated his responsibility. It was a dereliction of his duty to God. However, by creating a storm and a near-shipwreck, God saved him. Jonas went to Nineveh against his own will and preached the gospel!

Joseph was unquestioning in his obedience. He did not understand anything. He married a pregnant virgin and practiced celibacy for the rest of his life. He died before Jesus started his public ministry. Unlike Jonas,

Joseph obeyed unconditionally. He, in his simplicity, trusted God with all His paradoxes.

We have the option to become Jonas or Joseph. The choice is ours.

GO TO JOSEPH (ITE AD JOSEPH)

Long, long ago, a severe famine affected the land of Egypt. People cried out to Pharaoh: "Give us food to eat." The good old Pharaoh replied, "Go to Joseph, and do whatever he tells you." The Egyptians went to Joseph, and he fed them with the food stored in the granaries of Egypt.

Today when we starve spiritually, we cry out to God "Give us food." The church replies "Go to Joseph." Joseph, the foster father of Jesus, was the custodian of Jesus, the Living Bread. Joseph will direct us to his son, Jesus. Jesus himself is the Living Bread. He gives Himself to us in the Holy Eucharist.

In the present times, we need Joseph more than any other time in history. The church is falling prey to secular ideologies and political correctness. Confusion is rampant and heretic statements from the catholic hierarchy has become the norm. How do we remain sane at times like this? The answer is, "Go to Joseph."

JOSEPH IN EGYPT, JOSEPH
OUT OF EGYPT

It is interesting to see the similarity between Joseph, the Patriarch, and Joseph, the spouse of Mary. Long, long ago, Joseph the Patriarch escaped from death by going to Egypt. He became the Prime minister of Egypt and brought the sons of Israel to Egypt. He told the sons of Israel to take his bones out of Egypt on the day of their exodus from Egypt. Four hundred years later, Moses took the bones of Joseph from Egypt and led the exodus of Israelites out of Egypt. Figuratively speaking, it was also the day of Joseph's exodus out of Egypt!

Centuries later, Joseph, a descendant of David, led Mary and Jesus to Egypt. It was to avoid another death. This time king Herod wanted to kill Baby Jesus. Later, Joseph led Jesus and Mary out of Egypt. This was to fulfill the prophecy "I called My Son out of Egypt."

Joseph is the guardian and protector of the Catholic Church. He is asking us to come out of the bondage of Egypt. The bondage of Egypt is nothing but the bondage of sin.

JOSEPH THE DREAMER

Joseph the Patriarch was called "The Dreamer." Joseph saw prophetic dreams, and his dreams came to pass. Centuries later another Joseph came to the stage, and like Joseph, the patriarch, he also saw dreams. Joseph, the foster father of Jesus, saw dreams and he acted upon his dreams. His dreams and visions warned about future dangers, and Joseph avoided those dangers by taking prudent actions. His actions saved Jesus and Mary. He protected the Holy Family!

In an era characterized by outright onslaught on family values, we need the powerful patronage of Saint Joseph to protect each and every family from diabolical attacks.

THE EYE OF THE STORM

It looks as if Joseph was always amid a storm. Joseph was betrothed to Mary and was soon caught up in a typhoon. He found that Mary was pregnant and had to go through many nail-biting sleepless nights! It took a visit from the angelic envoy from heaven to clear the doubts of Joseph. He was relieved. The storm abated, only to be followed by another storm. He had to take the fully pregnant Mary to Bethlehem for the purpose of census. No one gave Mary a place to deliver the baby. Joseph was flustered. Eventually, after knocking on many unfriendly doors, the doors of a manger opened for them. The storm calmed down for a while. Joseph took a breath of relief, but when he hit his head on the pillow, another heavenly messenger told him to run to Egypt with Jesus and Mary. Now Joseph is caught in a category 5 hurricane! He crossed the barren, unfriendly, desert infested with vipers and wild beasts before reaching Egypt. With great difficulty he found work as a carpenter and fed Mary and infant Jesus. He learned the Egyptian language and befriended the Egyptians, but then the order came from heaven to leave Egypt. Poor Joseph is on his feet again. He finds job in Nazareth and builds a small house for Mary and Jesus. Fast forward, Jesus is twelve years old, and Joseph takes him to Jerusalem. On the way back, he finds that Jesus is missing. The next 3 days were successive days of emotional tornadoes for Joseph. Eventually when he found Jesus in the temple, his mind settled.

We do not hear anything about Joseph after that. It is believed that this righteous man who weathered many storms died before Jesus started his public ministry.

FATHERHOOD OR "OTHERHOOD."

Fatherhood has been killed or mutilated by a thousand cuts, more so since the sexual revolution. Fatherhood and motherhood have taken the backstage as the contagion of cultural communism has infiltrated Christian homes like a cancerous growth. Fatherhood has now become "Otherhood."

Families are decimated. The custodians of the church are turning a blind eye to this scourge. Theologians and politicians are talking in the same language, and confusion is rampant.

We were warned by the Fatima visionaries that the final battle between Jesus and Satan will be on the sanctity of marriage and family. We are seeing this battle happening right before our eyes. (Reference: The True Story of Fatima, John de Marchi, Fatima Center, NY, U.S.A)

JOSEPH AND THE FIRST DOMESTIC CHURCH

The Vatican II proclaimed that a Catholic family dedicated prayerfully to Christ can be called a "Domestic Church." The father, mother, and the children who live and walk with Jesus Christ constitute the domestic church. The head of the first domestic church was St. Joseph. In his house was Mary, the mother of God, and Jesus the Son of God. However, both Mary and Jesus depended on Joseph for food, shelter, and clothing. It was the hand of this simple carpenter that built the first home of Jesus. It was this man who taught Jesus the simple Jewish prayers of his time. Joseph built houses and furniture to earn a livelihood, and with his daily wages fed the Holy Family.

History repeats. There is a reflection of Joseph in every father, and there is a semblance of Mary in every mother. Paraphrasing John the Baptist, one could even say that a praying family is a domestic church where "the members of the family become smaller and smaller while Jesus grows bigger and bigger" day by day. Eventually the whole family will start developing a resemblance to the Holy family.

JOSEPH AND THE HOLY TRINITY

St. Joseph was selected to become the foster father of Jesus from among the procession of all created men since the beginning of the world. It was indeed a unique privilege bestowed upon Joseph by the Blessed Trinity. God the Father endorsed Joseph to become the father-figure of Jesus during his earthly sojourn. God the Son, called Joseph "father" during his earthly life. God, the Holy Spirit, entrusted Joseph with his dearly beloved spouse Mary. Clearly, Joseph was pleasing in the eyes of the Father, Son, and the Holy Spirit!

What made Joseph well pleasing to the Blessed Trinity? We do not know. We, however, know that Joseph occupies an exalted position in the heavens.

WHEN A MAN CICUMCISED GOD

Can you imagine or comprehend the fact that a mortal man was given the authority to circumcise God? Joseph decided to circumcise Jesus, the Son of God!

Joseph must have presided over the circumcision of Jesus on the eighth day as per the Jewish law. The Son of God obeyed the will of this simple carpenter from Nazareth. Like Abraham placing his son Isaac on the altar, Joseph must have placed little Jesus on a small stone altar for his "first sacrifice." It was the first time that the Son of God shed his blood. It prefigured the great sacrifice of Calvary

Baby Jesus must have cried like any human child. It must have taken many days for the wound to heal. Jesus must have given Joseph and Mary many sleepless nights from his incessant crying during the convalescence period.

This speaks volumes about the humanity of Jesus. Though He was the Son of God, He was also truly the Son of Man. He bled. He cried. He hungered and thirsted like any child, and thereby identified with every human experience.

THE BUDDING ROD OF AARON. THE BUDDING ROD OF JOSEPH

There are similarities between Old Testament and New Testament characters in the bible. It is interesting to watch these strange coincidences, and they are not accidental in their occurrence. For example, when the priesthood of Aaron was challenged by the Israelites,

God instructed the leader of each tribe to bring a staff. They were instructed to leave the staff in front of the Ark of the Covenant. The next day Aaron's staff sprouted, blossomed and produced almonds and God instructed Moses to put Aaron's staff in front of the Ark, as a permanent testimony to Aaron's priesthood.

There is a strong tradition that when Virgin Mary was of marrying age, the High Priest asked the men of the house of David to put a staff on the altar. Joseph was one among them. It is said that the staff of Joseph bloomed, and a dove descended on Joseph's head. It was taken as a sign that Joseph was to become the spouse of Virgin Mary. It is not mentioned in the Bible but is held as a powerful belief among Catholics.

What does this mean? Joseph represents the "Man of the house," and therefore is the "Priest of the House of Nazareth." Again, Catholics believe that Virgin Mary is the living Ark of the Covenant. Joseph standing before Mary is therefore akin to Aaron standing before the Ark of the Covenant.

THE PRIESTHOOD OF MAN

St. Joseph exemplifies the priesthood of man in the house. Even though Joseph was only the foster father of Jesus, God communicated with Joseph about all the major decisions in the family. God communicated to Joseph that the Son of God must be named Jesus. The angel informed Joseph to move the family to Egypt. Again, heaven communicated to Joseph to move back from Egypt to Nazareth. Virgin Mary is the mother of God and is more exalted in heaven that St

Joseph. However, Mary is not a priestess and she cannot do priestly functions. The order of Heaven is immutable irrespective of what human philosophers or theologians argue. The Catholic Church is undergoing a modernist metamorphosis for the worse, one must hold on to the wisdom of the saints and to the word of God to make sense of the truth in the midst of rampant confusion.

JOSEPH, THE DEFENDER

In the litany of St. Joseph, he is invoked as the terror of demons. Why is he called the terror of demons and the defender of the church? Clearly, Joseph was the protector and defender of the Holy Family, and therefore he must have been endowed with many graces. King Herod, an archetype of the destructive demon, wanted to eliminate baby Jesus. However, Joseph saved Jesus from this evil. If the Son of God depended on Joseph during his earthly life, how much more we must depend on Joseph for protection against demonic oppression? I cannot avoid a smile when I recall an incident that happened some time ago. It is quite funny. I use a voice recognition technology called "The Dragon" to dictate patient notes. When I dictate, the dragon software recognizes my voice and types it for me. One time the dragon quit working, and I called the Information technology software crew to fix the problem. They found that the essays I wrote about St. Joseph, under the heading "Joseph, the son of David' somehow disabled the dragon software. I wondered, "Is Joseph slaying the dragon?"

Joseph is the dragon-slayer and the defender of the mystical body of Christ (the church).

ESTHER AND THE KING, JOSEPH AND THE PHARAOH

We see parallels between Old and New Testaments. In the Old Testament when evil men plotted to eliminate the Jews through ethnic cleansing, God raised a simple Jewish maiden named Esther to save them. Esther won the heart of the Persian emperor and curtailed the evil plans of the Jew-haters of her time. Church fathers compare Esther to Virgin Mary. Virgin Mary won the heart of God, the king of kings, and protected the human race from the devil

Joseph the patriarch won the favor of pharaoh, and thereby ensured the safety of Jacob and his children. In a similar way, St. Joseph won the heart of God, the great King, and ensured the safety of his people. Joseph is still honored in the heavens as the earthly father of Jesus Christ, and therefore we have an ally in Joseph. The celestial court listens to the intercession of St. Joseph.

JOSEPH IN DORMANCY

It is interesting to note that devotion to St Joseph remained dormant in the church for a thousand years. No spoken word of this simple man is recorded in the Bible. Mostly we read about Joseph in relevance to his dreams. Similarly, he remained silent in the church for a millennium. It was only in 1129 that a church was dedicated in honor of St. Joseph. The church was in Bologna.

Like many other things, the church also goes through periodic quickening and awakenings. The church woke up from its slumber and welcomed Joseph only after the passing of a thousand years. God only knows why it took such a long time for the church to publicly venerate St. Joseph.

WHEN JOSEPH DREAMS

For some reason we see that the biblical character with the name Joseph are often mentioned as dreamers. When we start with Joseph the Patriarch, we see that he used to see dreams, and often boasted about it to his own detriment. It was the jealousy fueled by a prophetic dream that led Joseph's brothers to hate him with a perfect hate. The jealousy even turned into a murderous plot that was only averted at the last minute. Eventually, Joseph's siblings sold him to foreign merchants as a slave. We read again how Joseph saw prophetic dreams about the future of Egypt, and how by acting upon it saved Egypt from a great famine.

Centuries later we see another Joseph emerging from the pages of the Bible. It was none other than Joseph, the foster father of Jesus. The story of Joseph is essentially told through the four dreams that he saw, and how those dreams changed the life of boy Jesus.

JOSEPH, EGYPT, AND THE CONCEPT OF THE FIRST BORN

We know from the New Testament that St. Joseph went to Egypt with Mary and Jesus and later returned to the land of Israel. The evangelist even uses an ancient Old

Testament prophecy to substantiate this event. He says that this happened to fulfil the prophecy "I called my son out of Egypt." One cannot miss the striking similarity between this event and the story of Joseph the patriarch. Joseph the patriarch led his siblings and Jacob, his father, to the land of Egypt. The children of Jacob (The Israelites) lived in Egypt for centuries as slaves. Eventually Moses confronted the Pharaoh and said, "Thus says Yahweh, Israel is my firstborn son; and I say to you, let my son go that he may serve me." Clearly God is calling Israelites, the first born. Later Jesus is called the first born on many occasions. We know that Jesus being God was not created. He was called firstborn in the sense that he had preeminence in everything. The Israelites, the first born, were led to Egypt by Joseph the patriarch. Jesus, the first born, was led to Egypt by St. Joseph. It was Moses who led the Israelites out of Egypt. However, figuratively Joseph the patriarch went before them, because the Bible says that Moses took the bones of Joseph with him as per the explicit instruction of Joseph when he was alive. Joseph instructed the Israelites when he was alive, "God will surely come to your aid, and then you must carry my bones up with you from this place." (Exodus 13:19). Symbolically, the carrying of Joseph's bones out of Egypt suggests that he led Israel out of Egypt. St. Joseph on the other hand led Jesus out of Egypt

We see that the story of the immigration of Israel, the first born to Egypt, and its final exodus out of Egypt, was only a shadow of the things to come. Jesus, the real first born would later go to Egypt and come out of Egypt. Both these episodes are associated with the name of Joseph. Was it a coincidence or a God-incidence?

DEAR FATHER JOSEPH, DID YOU EVER CRY?

Dear Saint Joseph, did you ever cry? Did you ever lament? The Bible does not answer this and hence I ask this question to you.

I feel you have felt mental anguish and pain many times in your life. You were the head of the family. You were the bread winner. You might have felt terribly sad when Mary had no place to deliver. People complain about little things today. You never complained but held that pain in your heart. You might have wondered, "Why Lord, why. I couldn't provide your son with a decent place to live." You had to look at your son with pain on that cold December night when you couldn't provide even a blanket to cover his sacred body. He was covered in swaddling clothes instead.

You had to run to Egypt in the middle of the night like a fugitive. The land was hostile, and the weather was harsh. You had the guilt and fear that any man must face in such situations. You had to take your wife who was still a teenager along with her divine infant to an unknown land with strange customs. You had to transplant your vulnerable family from the land of comfort to the land of the gentiles. How many days did it take you to reach Egypt? Did baby Jesus fall ill on the way? How many times did you feel guilty while looking at the beautiful face of your beloved spouse? Where did you all sleep on the way? Did you have money to sleep in an inn? Did the Egyptians treat you well? Did you feel vulnerable in Egypt? How did you feed your spouse and your son? Did you ever question God?

How did you feel when the son of God worked as a carpenter? Did you feel guilty that you couldn't provide enough for your son and his mother? Did you feel inadequate when you had to keep Jesus to help you in your shop rather than sending him to study the law?

Did you ever think that God is punishing you for some reason, when you lost Jesus in the temple? Was your manliness hurt when you thought about your inability to protect your son? How did you go through the daily chores knowing that you are feeding the "bread of life" and the "ark of the covenant"? Oh! Blessed Joseph, how did you find favor with God, that he decided to send the word incarnate to your little house in Nazareth? How did you find favor to become the chaste husband of the mother of God?

Father Joseph, how should we honor you? Are we honoring you enough? Sometime when you have the time, answer my question. You know, I believe in the communion of saints.

ASK JOSEPH TO PREVENT DIVORCES

I have heard people asking St. Joseph's intercession for many things, but not to avert a divorce. Joseph contemplated divorcing his wife Mary. Joseph was betrothed to Mary, but to Joseph's dismay she was found to be pregnant. He was quite distressed and secretly contemplated divorcing his wife. He had every right to do so. If he applied the Law of Moses on her, she could have been stoned publicly. However, Joseph did not want to create a scandal, and therefore quietly decided to divorce her. Mary did not tell Joseph that the child was born of the Holy Spirit. However, the angel of the Lord let Joseph know that the child was born of the Holy Spirit, and therefore is the incarnate Son of God. Joseph therefore took Mary home as his wife.

Divorce is rampant and with divorce comes bitterness. Why can't we ask Joseph to intercede for those who are contemplating divorce?

JOSEPH, HOPE FOR A PITILESS UNIVERSE FORMED OF BRUTAL MATTER

I was reading about a singer recently. Apparently, she wakes up every morning with existential angst. She sings and writes to escape her existential void. If you take away love and joy, then universe is nothing but a pitiless place that holds brutal matter. There is no hope, faith, or charity. It is a dark world with no guiding star. It is a selfish world inhabited by self-loving intelligent brutes whose only aim is to dominate and exploit the weak. After all, they believe only in one religion: the religion of evolutionary biology. The doctrines of that religion states that the world is overpopulated, and that people are created with differences. This compels them to compete. The fittest

41

will survive, and nature selects them. Therefore, there is no place for taking care of the sick or reaching out to the marginalized. Such a world is a mini-hell. But if we think that we are all descendants of Adam and Eve and that God is our Father and Mary is our mother, then all of a sudden, this pitiless universe becomes a better place to live. Joseph was the earthly father of Jesus, and therefore he is our earthly father too. An awareness that we are not orphans in this world and that we are the children of God elevates us to a higher level of joy. Joseph, Mary, and Jesus can help us in this process.

DONUTS AND DIVORCES

When I was working as a physician in UK, I heard news of a senior consultant Gynecologist marrying a young midwife half his age. People were talking about the magic of donuts and its effect on marriage. Apparently, the charming midwife used to bring donuts for the aging gynecologist. The donut time with the midwife evolved into a romantic time for the doctor who was already bored with his wife. When the time was ripe the midwife asked the doctor to divorce his wife and marry her. She insisted that the marriage should be in an Anglican cathedral. The physician divorced his wife and married the midwife. He even neglected his children from the previous marriage.

What is the value of a marriage? It looks as if donuts can break marriages. Perhaps peanuts or chocolate can break marriages. Flattery can break marriages-the list is unending.

In all these situations, a man needs core-character values to deflect the subtle attacks on the marriage. The best and easy way to do this is by imitating Joseph, the quintessential husband.

A CITY WITHOUT SACRIFICE

I live in Peoria, Illinois, a very Catholic city with many churches. I used to boast to my friends and family that Peoria is the best city as it offered multiple confessions, masses and even perpetual adoration. There was confession and 7AM, 8.30 AM, 11.30 AM and 4.30 PM on a daily basis in various churches. There was mass in the morning, noon and evening. There were 2 churches offering 24-hour perpetual adoration. On the 13th of March,2020, following the outbreak of corona virus, all mass and sacraments were cancelled in this city. The churches are empty! This is something that I thought will never happen in my lifetime. But it happened. The daily public sacrifice of the mass has been abolished during the lent of 2020. Lent should be the time for repentance and the reception of daily sacraments. It is almost like the time of Jeremiah when the Babylonians destroyed the temple and abolished the daily sacrifice.

This is the time when one should put much emphasis on "Family, the domestic church." Families must huddle together and pray. Our model is the Holy Family of Nazareth. With St Joseph as our model and leader, we must pray the daily rosary, the litany of Loreto, and recite the chaplet of mercy to avert divine judgement.

PRAYER AT THE TIME OF CORONA EPIDEMIC

The world is living in fear. There is lockdown everywhere. Every religious gathering, including the mass, has been abolished. I was listening to an old Malayalam prayer. It was a prayer that my wife used to recite along with her grandmother. It is a Syrian Orthodox Jacobite prayer. I liked it and therefore translated it into English. I think it is a good prayer for difficult times like this. In Malayalam it is called **"Pattangapetta Daivam Thamburane."** The prayer is as follows,

Save us Lord
From all evil
From adulterous thoughts
From all enemies
From those who betray while pretending to love us
From the temptations of the devil
From the evil that proceeds from the wicked
From perverted emotions
From adulterated desires
From satanic thoughts
From corrupted dreams
From the hidden snares
From subverted words
From dereliction of duties
From all earthly temptations
From sudden death
From chastisements
From rage
From hatred
From lightning and thunder

From pestilence
From the fiery hell
From hardened evil deeds
From the worms that do not die
From the inextinguishable eternal fire
From weeping and gnashing of teeth
From bitter consequences
From the evil hour
From the evil hand that persecutes
From famine and fear
From emotional instability
From intolerable punishments
From the dreaded pronouncement from the Lord
"I do not know you, depart from me you wicked one."
From everything that separates us from the Lord
Save us Lord, Amen

JOSEPH IN HIS WORKSHOP

Bible testifies to the fact that Joseph was a carpenter, and that Jesus subjected Himself to His parents. Therefore, it is quite possible that Jesus worked as an apprentice in his father's workshop. Joseph lived in an agrarian society and the tools that he made were probably for farming purposes. Jesus used farm equipment as symbols while explaining the mysteries of the kingdom of God

I am sure Jesus would have thought about the yokes he made in His father's workshop when he said, "Learn from me, for my yoke is light." He would have thought about the ploughs that he made for the farmers of Nazareth when he said, "No one who puts his hand to the plow and looks back **is** fit for the kingdom of God." The memories of working in the carpentry shop of his father must have been fresh in the mind of Jesus, when he walked around ancient Palestine teaching about the Kingdom of God.

ONLY JOSEPH COULD HAVE DONE THAT

Imagine the plight of a man called to become the foster father of God, and the husband of a virgin who is the biological mother of God! As a man it sounds scary to me. No wonder the angel told Joseph not to fear. God, though a baby, is still God and probably even knew the thoughts of Joseph. Mary is born without sin and is absolutely free of sin. Both Jesus and Mary are "dangerously holy." How can you live day in and day out with such people without offending them? Joseph must have been extremely brave and holy to take up this assignment, which no man in history was ever asked to do.

If we realized who Joseph really was, then we would not have stopped thanking him even for a minute.

FAMILY IS THE NUCLEUS AND INDIVIDUALS ARE THE ATOMS OF THE SOCIETY

Family is the nucleus of the society and everyone is an atom. If you disrupt the nucleus or the atom, society will disintegrate. We are seeing the destruction of families, and the splitting of the atoms in postmodern Western civilization. Ancient Catholics prayed to the Holy Family, and entrusted their lives to Jesus, Mary, and Joseph.

Jesus, the Son of God, did not stay in an ethereal sphere disconnected from family or people. He subjected himself to a man named Joseph and depended on a woman named Mary. Even as an adult he stayed with his parents and helped his father and mother with the daily chores. He had cousins, and many of his disciples were his own cousins. Clearly, he was teaching us the value of family, faith, and friends. The agrarian society valued family, but rapid industrialization turned people into robots. We became detached from our roots and became cogs in a giant cogwheel. The universe became a heartless giant machine, and God became a disinterested watchmaker. The watchmaker is not interested in the watch once the watch is made, thus argued the agnostics of the last century. Rampant individualism destroyed tradition, custom, and community.

In the book, Return to Order (York Press, York, Pennsylvania,2013), John Horvat II argues that if individualism turned people into isolated atoms, its postmodern mutant split the atom itself. Classic individualism destroyed tradition and custom but postmodern individualism destroyed internal structures like logic, identity, and unity for the sake of instant gratification. He hypothesized that postmodern individualism "liberated" man from logic by fragmenting the unity of thought. This postmodern phenomenon deconstructed identity and even questioned nationality, sexuality, and personal name. In his opinion, this aversion to self-constraint led postmodern man to drugs, promiscuity and online fantasies.

We must search and actively fight to regain the ancient values of family, faith, tradition and God or else we will soon become colorless, odorless, tasteless, shapeless and lifeless mass of zombies. The answer is in imitating the Holy Family, under the patronage of St. Joseph.

FROM PERVERSITY TO PERFECT CHASTITY-THE STORY OF EXODUS

We all know the story of Exodus, and how God delivered Israel from the political oppression of Egypt. However, along with the political exodus, a spiritual exodus was happening. The spiritual exodus was what mattered to God, because he was cleansing a perverse people through centuries, so that they will be fit enough to receive the Messiah.

The ancient Israelites who lived in Egypt imitated the lifestyle of the Egyptians. They worshiped idols and engaged in lewd sexual behaviors. It is clear from their behavior at the foothills of Sinai that they were idolaters who attributed glory to a grass eating ox rather than to the Living God who saved them from Egypt. Adultery, incest, sodomy, and bestiality were common as these Egyptian slaves aped the immoral standards of their Egyptian masters. No wonder Moses pronounced curses on people who practiced lewd sexual behaviors. Down the centuries, God used prophets, priests and even kings to correct the immorality prevalent among the Hebrews. He used pestilence, famine and the enemy sword to correct their immorality.

Polygamy was practiced by the kings. Gradually Israelites understood the glory of monogamy and purity to the extent that this race of chosen people produced Mary, the woman without sin, and Joseph the chaste husband of hers.

God succeeded in this spiritual cleansing, and I say this because only the chosen people could have provided us with the perfect parents of the Messiah.

ESTHER AND MORDECAI, A TYPOLOGY OF MARY AND JOSEPH

In the story of Esther, she is mentioned as a cousin of Mordecai. Esther lost her parents at a tender age, and Moredcai adopted her as his daughter. Mordecai used to see prophetic dreams warning him about imminent dangers. It was a time when Jews were living in a foreign land and were subjected to many persecutions. It so happened that the king of Persia was displeased with his first wife Vashti and wanted to marry a virtuous virgin. He loved Esther, more than all other women and made her his queen. We know from the book of Esther how she saved the Jewish people from total annihilation by pointing out Haman, the deceiver, to the king. The king hung the deceiver and proclaimed that Jews were safe in his kingdom.

Mordecai is a typology of Joseph and Mary is a type of Esther. Both Mary and Joseph were from the same tribe and some church fathers even believe that they were related. Joseph, like Mordecai, used to see prophetic dreams about imminent dangers. He protected Mary, almost like a tender loving father. Under the protection of Joseph, Mary appealed the needs of her people (the Christians) to Jesus, the King of kings. We are living in a foreign land (the earth). Our real home is heaven. Haman is a symbol of Satan. Mary makes sure that Satan is crushed under her feet.

JOSEPH IN HEBREW MEANS "TO INCREASE."

Joseph was a common Hebrew name. The name literally meant "to increase." The great patriarch Joseph increased everything he touched almost like the proverbial Midas touch. He increased the produce and the granaries of Egypt beyond measure, even during the time of a terrible famine, that the neighboring people of Egypt came to Joseph for food. Likewise, Joseph the foster father of Jesus, provides us with the living Bread. Jesus is the living Bread, and Joseph safeguarded this life-giving bread in his powerhouse at Nazareth. Joseph stores up heavenly graces and treasures even today in the everlasting granaries of the kingdom of God. God, the Father says, "Go to Joseph", like the king of Egypt. When there was lack of food in Egypt, the Pharaoh told his people "Go to Joseph."

Joseph never fails anyone who comes to him. He not only provides, but also increases graces and treasures for his clients. He truly lives up to his name.

THE SINGULARLY CHAOTIC YEAR DOTTED WITH GRACES OF JOSEPH

Year 2020 began with chaos. Corona virus has become the grim reaper of Europe, Asia, America, Africa and

Australia. The ships are rudderless, the institutions are failing, economies are devastated, and nations are shaking. Millions have lost job all over the world. People are afraid. Hope is dying. The Holy Sacrament is denied. Even dead men do not get Christian burial. No one anticipated this calamity last year.

When there are no answers, I am turning to Joseph. When Herod killed the innocents, Jesus and Mary turned to Joseph for protection. Today, we must turn to Joseph for protection.

THE DIABOLICAL ATTACK ON FATHERHOOD

Extreme feminism attacked womanhood and motherhood to incomprehensible levels that childbearing and pregnancy are often considered like a malignant process while the elimination of the fetus is glorified as an act of self-liberation and emancipation. The next level of attack was on manhood, and we hear the academic intellectuals talking about "toxic masculinity" for any type of manly behavior irrespective of whether it is toxic or nontoxic. Political correctness and fear of retaliation led critical thinkers and moral theologians to cave in rather than confront this anthropologically incorrect conclusions on manhood and womanhood. Sexual liberation and gender ideology ran amok, and today men and women are totally confused. Men are not men anymore. Fathers have stepped aside, and husbands are not leading their families anymore. It is nothing short of total mayhem.

This is the time we need real father and husband figures like St Joseph to step in. He is the paragon of manhood and let us ask him to pray for families.

JOSEPH AND THE DESIRE OF THE EVERLASTING HILLS

Jacob, the patriarch, blessed his children individually. When he blessed Joseph, the patriarch, he promised him "the desire of the everlasting hills." What is the desire of the everlasting hills? The desire of the everlasting hills is none other than Jesus Christ, the incarnate God. Joseph, the patriarch, did not see Jesus. However, many centuries later another Joseph from the royal line of King David had the privilege of seeing, tending, training, and defending Jesus, the desire of the everlasting hills.

It looks as if the blessings of Jacob were preserved and reserved for centuries in the treasuries of heaven exclusively for St. Joseph.

WHY WAS JOSEPH AFRAID TO BRING MARY HOME?

In the Bible we read that Joseph was afraid when he heard that Mary was with child. The angel appeared to Joseph and told him "Fear not Joseph." Why was he afraid? Any mortal being with commonsense would have been terribly afraid in that situation. A man without commonsense or wisdom will not understand this, as he lacks knowledge of the supernatural realm. The image that comes to my mind is the petrified look on King

David's face on hearing the death of Uzzah. David was transporting the Ark of the Covenant on a cart and when the oxen stumbled, Uzzah reached out and took hold of the ark. God struck him down as he touched the ark of God without reverence. David was afraid on hearing this and said, "How can the ark of the Lord ever come to me?" Joseph, the descendant of David, understood that Mary was pregnant with the Son of God and was therefore the living ark of the covenant. For all the right reason, Joseph got scared. He had to show reverence to the mother of God, and for a brief period of time he went into a state of self-doubt and unworthiness that evolved into extreme anguish. The ancient ark contained the law and the manna, while Mary carried Jesus, the living manna and the fulfilment of the law. Joseph was literally repeating what David said before, "How can the ark of the Lord ever come to me?"

JOSEPH AND THE OFFICE OF THE DEAD

As a child I have seen older people invoking St Joseph's help for happy death. Later I realized that St Joseph is the patron of the dying. I did not understand why but assumed that it was one of those catholic traditions. In the St. Thomas Syrian Christian tradition (Syro-Malabar rite of the Catholic church) to which I belong, there is an elaborate office of the dead for the repose of souls. Ever since my younger days, I have participated multiple times in the office of the dead for dead relatives. It is sung in Malayalam by the priest and the people, and much of its content is from Psalm 130. In Malayalam it is called "Oppice", a Malayalam metamorphosis of the word "Office." It is an antiphonal psalmody performed by two choirs, singing alternate phrases from the psalms in melodious Malayalam. One group sing "out of the depths I cry to you, O Lord," and in reply the other group sings "O Lord, if you kept a record of sins, who could stand?" It continues back and forth, and the priest blesses the congregation and the tomb with holy water.

St. Joseph had a happy death as he died in the arms of Jesus and Mary. The logic is simple-if Joseph intercedes for us, Jesus and Mary will also come to our death bed and take us to heaven. Joseph is therefore considered the hope of the dying.

JOSEPH AND THE POWER OF SILENCE

I wondered when I started writing this book about the difficulty of penning about a man who does not speak even a word in the Bible. However, I knew that Joseph was a mystery of silence that needs to be unraveled and that the progressive unwrapping of this mystery will somehow benefit my soul. Cardinal Sarah in his recent book, The Power of Silence: Against the dictatorship of noise, talks about the mystery of silence and solitude. He says solitude is the best state in which to hear God's silence, and that God himself dwells in a great silence. He says that man must drape himself in deep silence to encounter God in the eternal silence in which he abides. It looks like the "theology of Joseph" to me. Somehow

Joseph knew this two-thousand years ago and practiced it more than anyone else. Today we have distracted ourselves with music, movies, TVs, smart phones, and the internet that we have no time to hear the silences of God. Therefore, we are confused beyond measure.

We need to learn about silence and solitude from St Joseph.

THE THEOLOGY OF JOSEPH AND THE INVERSE LOGIC OF FAITH

St Joseph is difficult to understand on cursory or superficial examination. One has to dwell on the inverse logic of faith to get a glimpse into his mind. We want to co-create a world through hard work, intelligence, social networking, accomplishment, power, competitiveness, raw ambition and passion, and these values go along with the material ethos of the contemporary culture. When we look at St. Joseph through the distorted lens of the current value system, he may appear to be weak or naïve. However, when we apply the inverse logic of Christian faith, everything about St. Joseph will fall into place. In the Christian universe, the poor in spirit inherit the kingdom of God. The meek shall inherit the earth, and the pure of heart will see God. In the Christian landscape the broken heart is the healed heart, those who lose life shall find life, and the last shall become the first. When we transcend into the alternate universe of Christian thinking, we come to the theophany of understanding that St. Joseph is very great in the kingdom of God.

JOSEPH, THE BULWARK

The song of Solomon says, "If she is a wall, we will build towers of silver on her. If she is a door, we will enclose her with panels of cedar." The wall and the enclosed door represent the perpetual virginity of the mother of God. Mary was a virgin before, during, and after the birth of Christ. If Mary is the wall, then Joseph is the silver bulwark surrounding her. If Mary is the closed door, then Joseph is the cedar panel that seals the door. Joseph is therefore the protector and the defender of the perpetual virginity of Virgin Mary. No wonder Joseph is called the terror of demons. Joseph had steely resolve in carrying out his job as the defender of the Holy Family.

We only have to ask Father Joseph, and he will come running to protect our families from diabolical attacks.

CAN ST. JOSEPH NEGOTIATE WITH KING HEROD?

Last year the Vatican entered a pact with communist China to assimilate the state sponsored "Catholicism" with the suffering underground Catholicism that remained faithful to Christ and its vicar despite unimaginable persecution. Cardinal Joseph Zen of Hong Kong repeatedly pleaded and begged with the Vatican to avoid this dreadful mistake. He asked, "Can you imagine St. Joseph going to bargain with Herod to save the infant Jesus?" There are forces in this world that are diabolically deceptive. The devil does not come with horns, tails, spikes and claws. If he came that way, we would have easily identified him. He is a sleazy seducer who comes as your benefactor. We need wisdom to discern his devious plot. Cardinal Zen knew it, St. Joseph knew it and many saints know it. However, the Vatican officials behaved like king Hezekiah who fell for the flattery of the Babylonian king and showed his envoys everything in his storehouse, treasury and armory. The enemy understood everything and later burned the temple to the ground, destroyed Jerusalem, and carried the Hebrews to Babylon in captivity. We should follow the example of St Joseph, and not Hezekiah, when we deal with the enemies of the church.

THE SCEPTER SHALL NOT DEPART JUDAH

God had promised that the scepter shall never depart Judah, but at the time of St. Joseph who was a royal descendant of Judah and David, the scepter of Judah had already passed into the hands of Herod, a non-Jewish Edomite. Joseph belonged to the Royal family of David but was a poor carpenter. God was not talking about an earthly scepter, but an everlasting scepter. Jesus, the son of Joseph, was to carry the eternal scepter in His everlasting kingdom. Jesus is the descendant of Judah and David, as he inherited that right from his foster father Joseph. Christ is the eternal king of the entire cosmos.

Jesus honors his earthly father even in his eternal kingdom.

JOSEPH AT THE THRESHOLD

I see St. Joseph standing at the threshold. He stands at the threshold between the Old Testament and New Testament, the Jewish law and the Catholic grace, Jerusalem and Rome, the temple and the church. He represents the end of an era and the beginning of a new epoch. He is the last link in the chain of Old Testament patriarchs. He ushers in a new order of grace. He links Judaism to Catholicism in a seamless manner. He is a Jew and a Christian, as he along with virgin Mary became the first Hebrew converts to Christianity. I therefore believe that St. Joseph has a special role in defending the Judeo-Christian moral ethos at a time of terrible moral upheaval.

DOWNWARDS AND OUTWARDS

The utilitarian world view tells us to use people as objects to meet our ultimate material end. It is all about self-actualization, independence, security, consumerism, brute force, and capital gains. However, we are not just matter and molecules. We have deep yearning for meaningful connections, sacrificial love, and a higher purpose in this existence. When we do not realize this higher calling, we drift into despair, depression, and a general sense of meaninglessness. This moral vacuum is responsible for suicide, substance abuse, violence, identity disorders, and the obliteration of families and societies. Instead of achieving this deep desire for meaningful connection, we go further and further into self-love. The vicious cycle continues.

The answer is to go downwards so that we can go outwards. We must go deep into our heart and soul to empathize with the heart and souls of fellow beings. When we see our insecurities, vulnerabilities, and brokenness then we will realize the existence of such emotions in others. We will become empathetic to fellow human beings. Such a person will literally branch-out and grow towards other people. He will become fruitful. The story of St Joseph is not of self-actualization, but of loving surrender. It is not about independence but about interdependence. Individualism and collectivism are replaced by the law of love. Joseph teaches us to love God with all our heart, mind and soul and to love each other like the way we love ourselves.

FROM DYSFUNCTIONAL MARRIAGE TO HOLY MATRIMONY

The Old Testament begins with a marriage that went terribly wrong, while the New Testament begins with the marriage par excellence.

The first man Adam turned out to be a simple fool. The first woman Eve rebelled and went after guilty pleasure, while at the same time dragging her unsuspecting husband into the same predicament. It ended in disaster. They lost paradise and communion with God. Their oldest son killed the younger one. We are all born with original sin because of this disobedient couple. However, the New Testament begins with a very Holy matrimony between St. Joseph and virgin Mary. They had the finest and most beautiful form of marriage whereby they entered into a fruitful and self-giving love that nurtured Jesus, the Son of God.

The Holy Family is the model for all families.

JESUS OF NAZARETH

Why is Jesus called Jesus of Nazareth? The answer is very simple: Jesus lived in the house that Joseph built in Nazareth. Jesus was born in Bethlehem because Joseph had to go there to register his name. Jesus spent his infancy in Egypt simply because his father Joseph took him and his mother to Egypt. My son Kevin was born in Karnataka state in India because I was teaching in a Medical school there at the time. Kevin lived in England for 7 years as I was working as a Physician in that country. Today his cousins call him Kevin of Peoria because he lives in Peoria, the town where I work.

In Malayalam language, Christians are called "Nazranis," simply because we follow the One from Nazareth. In time and eternity Jesus is known as Jesus of Nazareth solely because He lived in the house that His father built in Nazareth.

Jesus got his above designation entirely because of St. Joseph.

THE NAZARETH OF ENGLAND AND ITALY

The shrine of Our Lady in Walsingham, England, is called the Nazareth of England. Apparently, a Duchess in England had a vision of Mary who instructed her to build a house in the exact model and dimension of the house at Nazareth. This happened in 1061, and since then every English king and queen have visited Walsingham until it was destroyed by Henry VIII. It was again rebuilt in the 19th century. I visited this shrine first time in 1997on a pilgrimage from our parish church in Kettering, and subsequently went there three more times. The last time I visited the Nazareth of England was in 2003, just before leaving UK for USA. In 2014, I visited the miraculous house of Nazareth at Loretto, Italy. It is believed that the original house of Nazareth was miraculously transported to Loretto, Italy.

The house of Joseph at Nazareth is very dear to Jesus and Mary.

DOMINANT WILL, PASSIVE WILL, AND PARTICIPATORY WILL

I see three patterns in the way human will interacts with God's will. The first group thinks that God's will must adapt to their will. They behave like masters and expect God to carry out their errands. They imagine that they got everything right, and God is like a magician in the sky who is expected to behave like a Genie in the bottle. These are arrogant people who think that their indomitable will is what determines the behavior of God. In simple terms, they think they are gods. I see these types of "pastors" preaching prosperity gospels.

The second type has no will at all. They think, "future is written" and that fate cannot be changed. They do not have to work, change, or struggle as their future is written in their stars. They blame lifeless Jupiter, Mars, and Venus for their problems. They refuse to take responsibility, and they attribute everything to Karma, sins, and stars. They behave like helpless robots controlled by powerful alien forces. I see these types of people predominantly in the Eastern hemisphere.

The third group takes a middle path. They work, adapt, struggle, and plan their future. They change what they can, but still understand that there are circumstances beyond their control. They do their part in the best possible way and learn from their mistakes. They know that God is the author of history, but God works through people and does not treat people as robots. God created the human will, but He does not manipulate or dictate our will. He has given us a free will. We can choose right or wrong and thereby face the consequences of our choices. If we are willing to ask God for help, He is willing to help us step by step without ever intruding into our free will. God is a "gentleman" and not a tyrant. He will not barge in or break into our soul. On the contrary, He waits patiently outside our hearts. He is a benevolent father who is expectantly watching our moral growth. Our growth may involve suffering and pain, and He knows that his children develop character through suffering. When we gradually understand the loving will of our Father in heaven we, like children, will try to participate in His divine plan and become better human beings. I call this the "Participatory will." I believe saints are people with participatory will. St Joseph is the classic example of a man who participated in the divine plan of God.

IDOLS FALL WHEN HOLY FAMILY STEPS IN

The Holy Family lived as poor immigrants in Egypt. Egypt was a powerful and rich country with many palaces, pyramids, and temples. It is said that when the Holy Family moved into any Egyptian town, the idols in the nearby temples fell. We are the temples of the Holy Spirit, but often we have desecrated our temples with idols of money, prestige, power and sex. We must invite Jesus, Mary, and Joseph into our houses and hearts to get rid of these idols. The Holy Family will never fail us.

THE ALTAR OF ST. JOSEPH AND THE SACRAMENT OF MARRIAGE

St. Joseph was a married man, and he is aware of the challenges of marriage and fatherhood. Sadly, the Christian sacrament of marriage is breaking apart. Cohabitation without holy matrimony, divorces, and secular redefinition of marriages are all ripping apart the beautiful tapestry of married life. In 2014, I went on a pilgrimage to Rome, and I had the opportunity to attend Mass at the Altar of St. Joseph in St. Peter's basilica. I had the responsibility to read out the petitions during mass. There were petitions for world peace, peace among religions, healing of the sick and the poor. When these petitions were read out, the congregation enthusiastically joined me in prayer. There was another petition asking God to protect holy matrimony from the attack of secular politicians redefining marriage, and when this was read out there was pindrop silence for a minute, followed by an unenthusiastic Amen. I am still wondering why there was a silence. Is it because of political correctness, fear of rejection or denial of the catechism of the catholic church? I do not know.

THE VICAR AND LIEUTENANT OF THE ETERNAL FATHER

St. Joseph is the Vicar and lieutenant of the Heavenly Father. The Eternal Father is the ultimate father and all the graces of fatherhood comes from Him. In the procession of billions of men down the ages, the Eternal Father selected one and only one man to hold the unique position of the fatherhood of Jesus. Therefore, we must respect and honor St. Joseph with great devotion. He represented God, the Father, by nourishing, clothing, protecting, defending and training Jesus Christ. If Jesus needed Joseph this much, how much more we need him? He is our father, and the father of the mystical body of Christ (the church)

He defends us from diabolical spirits. He defends the church from heretics and immoral men.

ST. JOSEPH, THE SAINT OF THE THIRD MILLENIUM

It is interesting to note that St. Joseph is a late bloomer in Catholicism. It is strange that the man who represented the Eternal Father's role as a father-figure for Christ has remained silent in the Bible and in the church for centuries.

He voluntarily took the backstage and remained silent, true to his vow of humility. It took centuries for the church to unwrap the mystery of Joseph. It was in 1479 that pope Sixtus IV even introduced a feast for St. Joseph. Can you imagine that St. Joseph's name was not in the litany of saints until 1726? St. Joseph was made patron of the universal church only in 1870. Remember what Jesus said about the Kingdom of Heaven. He compared it to a pearl of great price that was found by a merchant who sold everything he had to acquire that single pearl. In a similar way, we must sacrifice many frivolous superficialities and search diligently to find St. Joseph, the pearl of great price. Gradually, we are nearing that pearl of inestimable value.

I believe that the third millennium will be the millennium of St. Joseph.

MALE CELIBACY IN JEWISH THOUGHT

When we read the Old Testament, we can see very clearly that the ancient Hebrews considered it an obligation for all males to marry and procreate. I wondered how in such a culture St. Joseph remained chaste against the norms and conventions of that society. I wanted to know the Jewish thoughts behind this. It was at that time that I had the opportunity to attend a few meetings of the Association of Hebrew Catholics, in St Louis. I liked the deep penetrating thoughts of the Jewish people who later became Catholics. Attending those sessions was like a breath of fresh air distinct from the false piety, pseudo humility and intellectual inferiority of the some of the "Cafeteria Catholic" clubs. I happened to get a booklet named "Born of the ever Virgin Mary," written by Dr. Anthony M.Opisso, and published by the Association of Hebrew Catholics, St Louis. Quoting Exodus 19:15, the author says that Moses, though married, remained celibate for the rest of his life after he received the command to abstain from sexual intercourse. There is a Jewish tradition that the seventy elders abstained from sex after their call. Elijah and Elisha were celibate. He says, "When for the sake of Torah, a rabbi would abstain from relations with his wife, it was deemed permissible for he was then cohabiting with the Shekinah (Divine Presence.)" The author also talks about the Zenu'im ("chaste ones") to whom the secret of the Name of God was entrusted as per ancient Jewish tradition. Therefore, it is clear that Joseph chose to remain chaste for the sake of the Shekinah of Jesus, and for the revelation and entrustment of Jesus, the Word of God.

THE GREAT EAGLE

Symbolically, a father figure is strong, fearless, protective and prudent like an eagle. There are many allegorical verses in the bible about eagles. Psalm 91 explicitly says "He will cover you with His feathers, and under His wings you will find refuge." Eagles are eternal enemies of serpents. The eagle represents the divine while the serpent represents the wicked, the reprobate and the damned. One can see rich and poetic metaphors when we read verses on eagles in the bible. Joseph, who represented God the Father on earth during the earthly sojourn of Jesus Christ, is like a great eagle with great wings, long pinions and plumage of many colors. He defended Jesus. He was prudent and quick in making decisions. He was wise. Under his watch Jesus and Mary thrived like the strong cedars of Lebanon.

St Joseph is the father of the church, and therefore I tenderly call him, "father."

THE JOSEPHITE MARRIAGE

Both St. Joseph and Virgin Mary had taken vow of chastity and they remained chaste throughout their marriage for a higher purpose. Therefore, the church calls it "the Josephite marriage." Exceptionally married couples have practiced this type of marriage, and the classical example is the marriage of Edward the confessor and Edith of Wessex. Old Testament prophets have used symbolisms to represent the virginity of Mary. They used metaphors like "Sealed Book," "Enclosed Garden," and "Shut East Gate," to describe the virginity of Mary. By extrapolation these symbols can be used to describe the virginity of St. Joseph as well. The chaste Josephite marriage represents the virginal marriage of the Church the bride, and Jesus, the Bridegroom.

THE ANGEL OF MARY, THE ANGEL OF JOSEPH

We see from scripture that angelic visitation was common in the life of Joseph and Mary. We know the name of the angel who visited Mary. It was a high-ranking angel named Gabriel, who was one of the seven angels serving the Most High God continuously before His throne. Gabriel addressed Mary with great reverence and announced to her that she was going to be the Mother of God. An Angel visited Joseph frequently in his dreams. We do not know the name of this angel, but in all probability, it was his Guardian Angel. The angel comforted Joseph and told him not to be afraid to take Mary home. The angel warned Joseph to flee to Egypt with Jesus and Mary to escape the wrath of king Herod. The angel also told him years later that Herod was dead and that he must return to Nazareth.

The angelic visitations in the lives of Joseph and Mary also teach us that we, the ordinary mortals of this world, are also surrounded by guardian angels.

THE MOST ROMANTIC COUPLE

I have lived in three continents and have seen all types of people. Immense volumes of literature are available on improving romance in marriage. Gurus, poets, experts, statisticians, theologians, sociologists, philosophers, and psychologists have analyzed and advised on improving romance in marriage. However, there is one vivid image of romance in marriage that has never left my mind. It was something that I saw in India when I was a twelve-year-old boy. I remember a poor man who worked in our coconut grove. He was tilling the soil, removing the weeds, and mixing manure and organic matter into the soil to help the trees grow better. I went there to see him working. It was summertime and the noon-sun was blazing in full glory above our heads. I looked across the paddy fields glistening in sunlight and spotted the figure of a woman afar. She was walking towards our direction. She was carrying a lunch box. Quarter of an hour later, she reached our site. The man told me that it was his wife. They smiled at each other and washed their hands. She spread a cloth over the grass and opened the lunch box. The aroma of the steaming fish curry and cassava has not left my nostrils yet. She put two plates, one for her and one for him, and served the cassava and the curry. They shared their happiness, concerns, and plans over the lunch, and they were so much in sync with each other that they were not even aware that I was there. After the lunch was over, she washed the plates and walked back to her humble abode on the other side of the paddy field.

I believe Joseph and Mary had a similar life: a simple, uncomplicated, and genuine love-life. Joseph worked as a carpenter in his workshop. Mary cooked, drew water from the well, and made attires for the family with her spindle, shuttle, and needle. In the evenings they prayed together and shared a humble meal. Romance in marriage is as simple that.

THE SWAN, THE CROW AND MY MOTHER

My mother was my fourth-grade teacher. I remember her teaching us the story behind the Malayalam poem "The swan and the crow." The Hindu mythology has recorded the life of a great warrior named Karna, who was born of a princess and brought up by a charioteer. He was constantly belittled and derided because of his "humble birth," as he was believed to be the son of a charioteer. Karna excelled in archery and martial arts, and while going to the battlefield, his own charioteer tried to demoralize him by telling the story of a well-fed crow competing with the royal swans. The crow ate the scraps that fell from the table and when he became fat, he challenged the celestial swan to fly across the lake. The swan tried to discourage the crow, but it did not work. Eventually, both decided to fly across the lake, and while flying the crow got fatigued and fell into the lake and died. The message is clear: Karna is the crow who is challenging the royal prince.

Jesus was mocked and belittled because of his humble birth. He is the king of kings and the lord of lords, but his own people tried to humiliate him by the calling him "the son of a carpenter." They thought Jesus would be ashamed of his roots, but on the contrary he was proud to be called the son of Joseph, the carpenter.

JOSEPH IN REM SLEEP

Our sleep goes through various cycles. We dream during the REM phase of sleep. It looks as if Joseph made all major decisions in his life based on REM sleep experiences. If you tell this to people today, they will ask: "What type of man makes decisions based on dreams?" Joseph accepted Mary based on a dream. He packed his bags and told the young mother to take her newborn and flee to Egypt following a dream. When things were going well in Egypt, he abruptly made decision to leave Egypt, again based on a dream. Acting purely on another dream, he decided to settle in the district of Galilee. Bible says angels communed with him in his dreams. How did he know they were angels, and not mere dreams or hallucinations? Surely, this man must have been unique to trust his dreams that much. History proved him right.

JOSEPH FED THE BLESSED SACRAMENT. WE FEED ON THE BLESSED SACRAMENT

Jesus, before He died on the cross, took bread and wine and declared that the bread was His body and the wine His blood. Then he told the disciples to eat his body and drink his blood and instructed them to do so. The 12 disciples celebrated this during their lifetime and by laying their hands on their followers, instructed them to continue the eucharistic celebration down the ages. For 21 centuries this has continued in apostolic succession, and today when the catholic priest says the words, the bread and wine become the body and blood of Christ. In mass we eat the body and drink the blood of Christ. But who sustained and nourished the body of Christ? Poor Joseph bought figs, olives and grapes for his son Jesus from the hard-earned money he got from carpentry. Mary cooked the food, and Jesus ate whatever was given to him by his parents

Today I can feed on the body of Jesus for the remission of my sins, because St. Joseph fed and protected Child Jesus.

ST. JOSEPH IN COMMUNIST CONCENTRATION CAMPS

There was an unknown bishop from Yugoslavia among the ranks of bishops in the second Vatican council. He was ridiculed and belittled by the learned bishops in the council. The Yugoslavian bishop's name was Petar Cule. Bishop Cule suffered terribly under the communists who sentenced him to eleven years of hard labor in concentration camps, and later put him along with other prisoners in a train that was purposefully wrecked. Because of the train wreck, his hip bones were shattered, and he walked with a limp for the rest of his life. He suffered anxiety and post traumatic stress disorder due to these unpleasant experiences. He had great devotion to St Joseph, and he pleaded nervously for the inclusion of St. Joseph's name in the canon of the mass. Bishop Cule believed that St. Joseph saved his life in the communist concentration camp. While Bishop Cule was talking, the rest of the bishops were mocking him. Unknown to everyone, Pope John XXIII was watching this on a closed-circuit television. The Pope personally knew the slow martyrdom of Bishop Cule and breaking all protocols, he included St Joseph's name in the canon of the mass with immediate effect. This incident is described in the book Consecration to St. Joseph, authored by Fr. Donald Calloway.

THE SANCTIFIERS OF HUMAN FAMILIES

Jesus, Mary, and Joseph were humans with body and blood. While Joseph and Mary were mere humans, Jesus was true God and true Man. By nature, all three of them were like us in their bodily functions. They did not sit on an ethereal cloud detached from the sweat and toils of human life, but rather went through every mundane activity of human life and sanctified it for us. Humans go through conception, intrauterine growth, motor and language development, and every bodily function before they grow old and die. Jesus, Mary, and Joseph also went through their respective bodily activities. A human fetus is sacred as Jesus sanctified every human fetus, by being a fetus Himself. Jesus died on the cross and thereby hallowed human death. He even consecrated our corpses by dying on the cross. Christians bury corpses with respect, because the body is the abode of the soul. Mary, the mother of God, glorified human pregnancy. She nursed and breast fed the Infant God. In a society that has devalued the female body, the model of Mary should give us hope. When "elites" look down on poorer people working as unskilled or semi-skilled laborers, the model of Joseph the carpenter, shines as a beacon of hope for those without hope. Jesus identified with the marginalized outcastes of our society by suffering along with them on the way to Calvary. Every human state and emotion have been elevated to the divine realm by Jesus, Mary, and Joseph.

Today, fatherhood, motherhood, and childhood are under diabolical attack and we must dedicate our fragile families to the Holy Family to prevent spiritual disasters in the future.

THE CAFETERIA CATHOLIC AND THE UPSIDE-DOWN JOSEPH

I have a Catholic friend. He is a good man and is very charitable. However, he is always politically correct, and carefully watches the popular opinion. He avoids talking about his faith though he goes to Mass every Sunday. He is one of those good souls who believes that faith is a private matter. He knows that I write Christian books, but I carefully avoid mentioning about my books or faith lest I offend his sensitive soul. He had to sell a house and so he got a statue of St. Joseph and buried it upside down in his yard. A few days later the house was sold at a good price. He did not tell me this, but my wife heard it from a mutual friend. I was amused. He is a practical man who knows how to use people, saints and religion to his advantage. I even wondered if I should learn from his practical wisdom and abandon writing about my faith to avoid trouble. God loves everyone, and I have no advantage financially or otherwise in writing this book. I write this book only because my heart is overflowing with these thoughts. I know I am not better than him spiritually because he is a righteous and charitable man. My wife asked me if I would bury St. Joseph upside down if I had to sell my house. I replied no. I could not bury the statue of a person whom I love in an upside-down manner. I told her that in such a situation I would ask for St. Joseph's intercession. If I had to bury his statue, I would bury it upright and not upside down. I am not taking a moral high ground here, nor am I pointing finger at him. I am just telling what I believe. Later, I realized that many Catholics and non-Catholics do this trick when they are about to sell their house. I am not condemning anyone; I am just expressing my opinion. I will not bury the statue of my father upside down, and by the same logic I will not bury the statue of Father Joseph upside down either.

MOLECULES OF WASTED LIVES

What is a wasted life? A life lived without ever knowing the agape love of the Living God or of the people around us, a life of extreme narcissism where the person loves himself and himself only to the total elimination of God and fellow beings, a self-worshiping will engrossed in pleasing every desire of the five senses, is what I call a wasted life. We are born to love, sacrifice, and to be loved in time and eternity. This life is only the steppingstone to the next. Everything is passing away like the wilting flowers in the meadows. Nothing is permanent. Only the transcendental soul is permanent.

We are wasted molecules of organic carbon if we refuse to accept the eternal perspective of our lives. We may have amassed political power, popularity, plenty of money and all forms of luxury, and in the process of doing so might have scapegoated and destroyed many innocent souls, but the cry of the innocent is incessantly before the throne of the eternal judge.

We must delve deeply into the "Theology of Joseph" to understand the true meaning of life or else we will be thrown into the garbage bags of eternity as wasted molecules.

JOSEPH AND THE "FATHER-WOUND"

Anthropologists, sociologists, and psychologists have observed a direct correlation between "fatherlessness" and the delinquent behavior of children. A father-figure may be absent physically or emotionally in the life of many who fall prey to lawlessness, pornography, domestic violence, and teenage pregnancies. Children get into gangs and cults when they come from a family where the father is emotionally distant from his children. Youngsters are wounded and yearn for the love of a father. As they have not seen a loving father-figure on earth, they have extreme difficulty in connecting with the Heavenly Father. Such people fall easily into existential angst. If we could somehow bring St. Joseph in that gap, then a transformation is possible. St. Joseph represents the Heavenly Father. How can you love an unseen God, without loving an earthly father made of flesh and blood? Joseph is a father to the fatherless, and thereby he gives a faint model of the unseen Heavenly Father. St. Joseph is the steppingstone and the Heavenly Father is the capstone. We need to see the concrete form before we can appreciate the abstract image. St. Joseph stands in the gap left by earthly fathers who have failed their children. By giving a model of fatherhood, he leads us gently to God, the Heavenly Father.

"DISSOLVE AND CONSOLIDATE"-THE MOTTO OF THE EVIL ONE

The Devil is the first rebel. Jesus says in the bible that Satan was a murderer and a liar from the very beginning. He is the hero of the wicked ones. He is the commander in chief of the revolutionaries and communists. What do revolutionaries and anarchists want? They want to destroy, annihilate, and dissolve the current order and then "recreate" a revolutionary disorder so that they can control every human being. In other words, these so-called elites want to have absolute power on human speech, thoughts, and movements. They want to usher in an era of total confusion. They have started this rebellion by turning women against men and intellectualizing that movement by calling it feminism. They also turned men against women by glorifying violent sex through free pornography and called it by the benign term, "adult entertainment." By turning the sexes against each other, they created a "Class-war" between husbands and wives. They encouraged rebellion in children, by creating gender ideologies. Furthermore, through contraception, abortion, and divorce, they exalted cultural communism. By doing so, they have effectively destroyed the family, the basic unit of any society. The damage has been done, but we can resist it to some extent by following the example of St. Joseph, the pillar of families. There is a reason why the catholic church has designated the tittle, "the pillar of families" to St. Joseph. St. Joseph, Virgin Mary, and Jesus have shown the absolute model for a holy family.

77

We must imitate them to protect our families from the deluge of immorality.

JOSEPH, THE TERROR OF DEMONS

I was not aware of this title of St. Joseph until I visited St. Joseph's oratory of Mount Royal in Montreal, Canada. In that basilica, I saw a powerful image of St. Joseph rebuking the demons. It makes sense that demons shudder at the name of St. Joseph, as he was the foster father of God-incarnate. Tradition has it that when Joseph, Mary and boy Jesus entered the towns of Egypt, the idols of Egypt fell from their pedestals. Joseph is pure and chaste, and demons cannot stand these virtues. In addition, the devil hates the quality of obedience. Joseph was obedient to the will of God throughout his life.

A long time ago when Joseph, the patriarch, lived in Egypt, he might have been the only man in the entire country to have known the God of Abraham. Everyone else in Egypt worshiped the pharaoh, Horus, Osiris, Isis and other pagan gods and goddesses. Centuries later St. Joseph visited pagan Egypt carrying the Son of God in his arms. Naturally evil spirits fear St. Joseph.

HE MADE HIM LORD OF HIS HOUSE AND RULER OVER HIS POSSESSIONS

In the Old Testament we see how the pharaoh made Joseph, the patriarch, the lord of the king's house and ruler over his possessions. It was only a shadow of the things to come. Many centuries later, the King of Kings made St.

Joseph the ruler of his house. Joseph was the ruler of the house at Nazareth that sheltered the Infant God and His Queen Mother. Joseph was the only man among all men to have the unique privilege of becoming the lord of God's home. His authority, sanctity and privileges are far above that of other saints, because he was the legal father of Jesus and the husband of Mary. He is above Augustine, Aquinas, Francis and Anthony because he was the Lord of God's own house.

"ONE BRIEF SHINING MOMENT"

The Americans know this quote well: "Don't let it be forgot that once there was a spot, for one brief shining moment that was known as Camelot." Jacqueline was referring to her late husband JFK when she quoted this song from the King Arthur story. (Reference: Life Magazine, Interview, December 6, 1963) The reign of David was a brief shining moment in the history of ancient Israel. There was never a time before or after, that equaled the glory of King David. The Kingdom of Christ was not in this world, but an everlasting heavenly kingdom and it cannot be compared to a mortal kingdom. David, the ruddy young man and the heartthrob of the Hebrew maidens, decimated the Philistines and established a great kingdom. Unfortunately, his descendants did evil before the Lord, and were taken captive by the neighboring Assyrians. Never ever did Israel regain its material glory. One obscure descendant of David, named Joseph, did capture shining glory not for a moment but for all eternity. Joseph's Son is the King of Kings, and he has glorified Joseph in all eternity. Surely,

Joseph is sitting on a high and mighty throne next his Son, Jesus.

ETERNAL FATHER VERSUS FATHER JOSEPH

Jesus explicitly indicated in the gospels that Virgin Mary is our mother. St. John the apostle who stood at the foot of the cross represented each one of us. Jesus looked at him from the cross and said, "This is your mother," and the bible says that St. John took Mary home. However, Jesus never said that St. Joseph is a father to all of us. So how can we assume that Joseph, the foster father of Jesus, is also our father? We can indirectly extrapolate it, though there are no explicit biblical commands on the fatherhood of Joseph. Jesus tells us to call God, the Eternal Father, "Our Father," in the Lord's prayer. As baptized Christians we become adopted children of God through the workings of the Holy Spirit. Jesus is the Son of God, but God the Father still entrusted Him to the care of Joseph, His earthly father. If the Son of God needed Joseph, we too will need him during our earthly sojourn. This is the argument on the fatherhood of Joseph.

FAMILY, THE NEW THEATER OF WAR

In the final apparition at Fatima on October 13, 1917, the final celestial event was that of St. Joseph blessing the world. St. Joseph appears only rarely in apparitions, unlike Virgin Mary who has appeared multiple times in the course of human history. I, therefore, wondered about the significance of the apparition of St. Joseph carrying Baby Jesus on the last day of the Fatima apparitions. Did Joseph know that twentieth century will bring dismal, dark, and diabolical attacks on human families? I think he knew that. The Holy Family appeared on the last day to declare solidarity with every human family. As predicted, families have become the new theater of diabolical wars. Fatherhood, motherhood and childhood has been decimated systematically by ultraliberal cultural Marxists in the last one-hundred years. St. Joseph is the pillar of families, and we need his intercession during these difficult times.

INTERGENERATIONAL BLESSINGS OF JOSEPH

St. Joseph is a historical figure, and so is Alexander the Great. Alexander came, saw, and conquered the world. He became the undisputed emperor of the world. He died when he was 33, and even today history books are flooded with his stories. He changed the world for ever and the effects of his conquest had far reaching effects in the annals of history. However, Alexander only existed in a brief span of space and time, unlike St. Joseph who lives in heaven even to this day. As St. Joseph exists in the heavenlies, he has a living presence today. He is therefore capable of imparting intergenerational waves of blessings in a continuum of time and space, unlike mere historical figures. Historical figures exist in history books, but St. Joseph is a palpable figure in the celestial realm. Alexander or Caesar cannot help me today, but Joseph can. That is the relevance of St. Joseph in the twenty-first century.

WHY DO KINGS WRITE? WHY DO KINGS SING?

Recently I had a conversation with my son about character and integrity. To illustrate the difference between character and human flaws, I asked him a question. I asked him if he considered King David, a man of character or not. He thought for a while and nodded his head in the affirmative. I asked him a rhetorical question. If David had no character, then why did God, the Father, call him "A man after My on heart?" Why is Jesus the Son of God described as the son of David? It is true that David had flaws. He committed adultery with another man's wife and even killed her husband. It was not a consistent bad behavior on the part of David, and after that incident he literally lived the life of a repentant sinner and wrote many penitential psalms. Even today, every sinner searches the psalms of David when he wants to explicitly speak an act of contrition to God. David wrote and sang to dissolve the clouds of guilt looming in his heart, and his psalms have been a healing balm to the broken hearts of millions of sinners over four millennia. What an accomplishment! God turned the flaws of David into gems of repentance. David was crushed internally and externally, and his crucible was tested in scorching fire. He came out victorious, and his victories and tribulations are recorded with great honesty in the Bible.

We all can learn from David, the ancestor of Jesus.

NINE NIGHTS, NINE HYMNS, AND NINE DIFFERENT TUNES.

My father was born into the erstwhile kingdom of Travancore in southern India. When India declared independence from the British in 1947, the kingdom of Travancore was assimilated into the Republic of India. The kingdom of Travancore was very forward in its thinking amongst the princely states of India. There were many great kings in Travancore, but here I am writing about a polymath and a polyglot named His Highness Swathi Thirunal Rama Varma, the Maharaja who reigned over Travancore for about 15 years. He was born in 1813 and died in 1846 at the age of 33. In this short period of time he formulated code of laws, courts of justice, and a manuscript library in Travancore. Furthermore, he introduced English education, modern Western system of medicine and health care, the first government printing press, an observatory and even a zoo. He was fluent in English, Malayalam, Sanskrit, Marathi, Telugu, Hindi, Kannada, Bengali and Tamil. He learned both Hindustani and Carnatic classical music systems and composed over 400 hymns and songs in various languages. He had a premonition that he would die young, and so surrendered his "King's sword" to God. He then instructed that the hymns he wrote must be sung for nine nights during the festival of Navarathri which celebrates the triumph of good over evil. He instructed that nine hymns composed by him must be sung in nine ragas(tunes) for nine nights. It is still sung in Trivandrum every year during the Navarathri festival.

Travancore was far advanced than other princely states at the time of Indian Independence thanks to Maharajas like Swathi Thirunal. Interestingly, the First Syro-Malabar Catholic saint named St. Kuriakose Elias Chavara who lived in the nineteenth century established a Catholic Printing Press in the model of the printing press established by Swathi Thirunal. The Saint took an expert blacksmith with him and went to Trivandrum. The blacksmith made a model of the government printing press of Swathi Thirunal and created the first Catholic printing press at Mannanam in Travancore, India. Saint Kuriakose Elias named the first printing press after St. Joseph. Even today, the printing press is called St. Joseph's Press, Mannanam, India. Many Catholic devotionals, biographies, and theological treatise were printed in Malayalam at that Press over the last three centuries.

St. Joseph may therefore be aptly considered the patron of the first Catholic Malayalam Press.

MEMORIES FROM A SCRAPBOOK

My children, with the help of my wife, made a scrapbook for me this year. They worked on it for weeks, meticulously arranging each photograph and other creative items like old cards and writings, in the carefully crafted pages of this scrapbook album. My daughter also did a nine-day novena for me and presented the scrapbook to me on Father's Day. The scrapbook was neatly arranged and creatively decorated. The theme of the second page of the scrapbook was about myself and my father, and it contained old photographs of me with my father. Interestingly enough, my daughter took a picture of the front page of my book Ninety-ninth step to my father's hill and incorporated it on that page. The theme of the third page was about my mother. It carried many pictures of my younger days with my mother, and my children surprised me again by putting the front page of my book A Tryst with Mary alongside my mother's picture. The other pages were about my children, my wife, my old friends, and about my days in India, UK and USA. What impressed me the most was the idea of incorporating God, the Father, and Virgin Mary, the mother, in the pages dedicated to my father and mother respectively. I was happy that my children were able to extrapolate the idea of fatherhood to God the Father, and motherhood to Mary the mother of God. It was obvious that they were not treating God as a distant, ethereal, and lonely being living somewhere in the distant skies. They knew that God is really a Father to us. In the same way, they figured out that Mary is really a mother to us, and that the adage that "Mary is our mother" is not an old cliché.

We are living in a disconnected vacuum of virtual realities and falsehoods that constantly create a feeling that "we are condemned to live" in a mechanical and hostile universe without love, beauty, or truth. In this existential abyss plagued with angst, people have lost belief in the Fatherhood of God and the motherhood of Mary. The world has sucked the sap of love out of us, and many people feel empty. This has created a notion that this world is void of love, goodness or compassion. Therefore, we are unable to see God as a Father. We think He is a malignant dictator or a "blind watch-maker." The moment we destroy this stronghold, a new vision is born. The new vision tells us that God is Father to us, and Mary is our mother. It is the magic moment of crossing from darkness to light, from ignorance to wisdom, and from death to everlasting life. Simply stated, we are not orphans in this world. We are still tied to God and His Mother through the unseen umbilical cords of love.

THE BLESSING OF THE WOMB AND THE FRUIT OF THE WOMB

It occurred to me yesterday, that I have been pronouncing blessings on the womb and the fruit of the womb, every time I recite the rosary. I never thought about the Hail Mary prayer that way. Every time we say Hail Mary, we proclaim "Blessed are though among women, and blessed is the fruit of thy womb, Jesus." It was a man named Joseph who maintained and protected the blessed womb of Mary, and the fruit of her womb, Jesus. Joseph and Mary are the paragons of manhood and womanhood, and therefore they represent every man and every woman. Hence, by extrapolation, it is the duty of every man to protect and bless the womb of his wife, and to bless and nurture the children born of those wombs. Unfortunately, men are becoming active agents in turning the wombs of women into the tombs of their children, by actively participating in abortion. Blood of innocent babies are shed in the wombs. Men have abdicated their responsibilities and have joined hands with evil social engineers and eugenic philosophers to usher in an era of pure infanticide. Million of humans are slaughtered in the wombs of their own mothers while men are bar hopping and beach partying like fossilized teenagers. We, men, need abundant grace, and St. Joseph should be our role model.

BUZZ WORDS AND DOG WHISTLE, THE PETRI DISH OF CULTURAL MARXISM

It is said that critical thinking is the science of morality. Without critical thinking, we diminish ourselves into a senseless tribal mob of animalistic zombies. In fact, every revolution was initiated by a mob. The French revolution, the Russian Bolshevik revolution, and the cultural revolution of Mao depended entirely on misguided, brainwashed mobs. Unfortunately, we are seeing the death of critical thinking in public discourses in America. Every critical thinker is booed down as a bigot who is intolerant and insensitive to the pain and passions of the people. Buzz words like bigotry, intolerance, colonialism, and racism are used to stifle dialogue. Real people with real souls are either reduced to the status of "fighting animals" or "trophies of martyrdom" by scheming politicians without an iota of morals to meet their political ends. The buzz words they use are nothing but dog whistles for elites dreaming of a new Marxist world order. My Neurology colleague is from China and has seen and lived through Mao's cultural revolution. He came to America to leave Mao's ideology, but seeing the recent developments in America he said, "It looks similar to the cultural revolution of China."

The answer is critical thinking. Critical thinking examines with an open mind what we normally take for granted, rather than buying into the lies, mottos, and agendas that stifle open dialogue and critical thinking in a democratic world.

THE FATHER RUNS FROM PILLAR TO POST, THE MOTHER SHED TEARS, THE SON SWEATS BLOOD

The twenty first century has brought fresh challenges to families. The common thread in every family drama is suffering. People cannot understand the meaning of suffering. In such situations we must look at the family par excellence which is the Holy Family. The Holy Family was not spared of suffering. Joseph literally had to run for his life from city to city, and from the country of Israel to Egypt and again back to Israel. He was not in any esteemed social position and had to work hard as a peasant to feed his family. Virgin Mary became the archetypical sorrowful mother by shedding copious tears at the foot of her Son's cross. Jesus, the Son of God, sweat blood. He was stripped of his clothes, flogged on a pillar, and humiliated all the way to Calvary. There, at the top of the hill, they nailed his flesh on a Roman cross. Dehydrated, defeated, and dripping blood; He died a slow and painful death.

Here is the cosmic question to us. Were Joseph, Mary and Jesus losers? Was their suffering a waste? There must be a meaning in righteous suffering, or else the Holy Family would not have suffered this way. Suffering has redemptive value. Therefore, God allows suffering.

JOSEPH IN THE DESERT. JESUS IN THE DESERT

We all know how Jesus was led by the Holy Spirit to the wilderness where He fasted and prayed for forty days. However, Jesus had a "desert experience" much before that. He was in the desert with Father Joseph when he was an infant. After the birth of Christ, Joseph was warned in a dream to flee Israel. Joseph, Infant Jesus, and Mary fled to Egypt to save their lives. They journeyed through the wild and inhospitable deserts of Egypt for many days, facing the threat of robbers, vipers, scorpions, and savage beasts. Many years later, Child Jesus faced the same desert experience while returning to Israel from Egypt. He therefore had a chance to observe the ways and means to survive in a desert from Joseph, his earthly father.

Israelites had to wander in the deserts for forty years. Prophets like Isaiah had to run to the desert to escape the wrath of Jezebel, the evil queen. The desert fathers lived in the deserts of Egypt meditating on the mysteries of Christianity. What makes these desert experiences unique? Why did patriarchs, prophets, mystics and theologians seek the wilderness? The Desert is a place of death and regeneration. It is also a place of

89

transcendence. It is the perfect battleground to control lust, greed, and pride. It is therefore a testing ground for sanctification. God, in His immense mercy, allows people to have physical or spiritual desert experiences to cleanse them and to make them strong.

Jesus Himself had watched Joseph go through his physical and spiritual desert experience, and it prepared Him for his own desert experiences.

THE STATE OF THE UNIONS

The state of the union of husbands and wives is in pretty bad shape. The current spiritual climate is not conducive for traditional marital and family life. There are many constraints in married life, and secular culture is moving away from ancient paths. The world is actively promoting alternate lifestyles. Intellectuals are replacing "insensitive and crude words" like adultery with benign and appealing words like "alternate lifestyles," "choices" and "modern families." These carefully crafted words are designed to make adulterous lifestyles appealing, desirable, and even sophisticated. People with a poor self-image may buy into this error to look acceptable to the "elites." Recently, a married celebrity who had an open affair with a younger man was calling the affair "an entanglement." See the use of word play in this situation. Sin can easily be normalized using word play. We humans excel in self-deception.

It is easy to lose focus in this culture. The social media and printed media are constantly bombarding us with "desirable alternate lifestyles." A lie told million times will give the appearance of truth, and for this reason we must search the scriptures to remain anchored to the truth. Joseph, Mary, and Jesus are the ultimate model of human family, and we must never take our eyes off the Holy Family.

THE DIGNITY OF LABOR

I heard the phrase "dignity of labor" for the first time from my eighth-grade teacher. She was emphasizing how every one's labor has inherent dignity, and that no one should be dismissed or belittled based on the work he does. It made great sense in India, at that time, as institutionalized caste system based on labor was prevalent in India. For almost four-thousand years, Indian civilization gave scriptural sanction to discriminate the two lower castes purely based on their work. The two lower castes people worked as merchants and peasants, and they were not allowed any social privileges. The English word pariah comes from the name of one of the lower castes in India. It is self-evident that a pariah is an outcast.

Ancient Israel also practiced prejudice and bias based on work. The "elites" of the day could not stand the wisdom or holiness of Jesus, and therefore they taunted him by calling him, "the son of a carpenter." Joseph was a carpenter. It is a common strategy practiced by sophisticated people in every age to belittle their opponents by attacking their humble roots. These men cannot defeat Jesus in debate, and therefore they punch him under the belt. Jesus however knew better. He came to sanctify every human experience, including human labor. Jesus himself worked as a carpenter before he launched his public ministry.

FORMULA: w=W=H

I have studied formulas and equations in science classes, but recently I read about a formula in Theology that works for holiness. The formula was proposed by St. Maximilian Kolbe to increase holiness among Franciscans. His formula is w=W=H. w stands for my will. W stands for God's will. H stands for holiness. According to St Kolbe, holiness is nothing but conforming our will to God's will (Reference: 33 Days to Morning Glory, Michael E.Gaitley). When we submit to God's will, we become holier. Jesus taught this in the Lord's prayer when He said, "Thy will be done." The classic example of this type of holiness is seen in the life of St. Joseph, who followed the instructions of God in everything he did. We, on the other hand, want God to obey our will. We get angry when our prayers are not answered because we think we know better than God. We say, "let my will be done." We want God to behave like a genie-in-the-bottle who carries out our whims and fancies. This is in opposition to the rule of holiness. The easy way to holiness is to study the life of St. Joseph and to follow God's will even when we do not comprehend it fully.

THE ROAD OF TRANSFORMATION AND TRANSCENDENCE

The Road to Egypt was an experience of transformation for Joseph and Mary. They learned many life skills and spiritual lessons on the desert road to Egypt. Interestingly, roads are also symbolically and spiritually a place of conversion and transformation. On the road to Emmaus, two disciples met the risen Lord, and it transformed their life forever. They learned the interpretation of the law and the prophets from Jesus himself, and understood in an irrevocable way the meaning of the Eucharist. Saul who hated Christians with a perfect hate became the beloved St. Paul of Christians on the road to Damascus. On the road to Milvian bridge, the pagan emperor Constantine had a conversion experience, and he became a Christian emperor. St. Ignatius of Loyola had a vision of God the Father and the Son at the curve or bent of a road in Rome called La Storta, and this led to a transformative experience in Ignatius and in Ignatian spirituality.

God is always speaking, even when we are walking or driving on the roads. The only question is "Are we listening to Him?"

WIFE, A FRUITFUL VINE. CHILDREN LIKE OLIVE SHOOTS

Psalm 128 talks about the attributes of a man loved by God. Such a man's wife shall be like a fruitful vine, and his children shall sprout around the table like olive shoots. Look at Joseph. Is there any man in history luckier than him? His wife Mary was the ultimate woman, the woman who was more than just a fruitful vine. She is the crown of creation, and no created being has surpassed her in beauty, charity, or truth. She is the Immaculate Conception. She is the mother of God. Despite all these unimaginable honors, she will still be known as the wife of Joseph in time and in eternity. Joseph was the foster father of God! Can you imagine, God depended on a carpenter for safety, shelter, food, and clothing. Joseph sheltered and nurtured God. Joseph is the most honorable man among the procession of men from Adam to millennials.

PRESENCE, ABSENCE, COVID-19, AND THE GREAT COMMANDMENT

COVID-19 has brought a subtle and oblique attack on the way we used to practice the great commandment. Most of us are worried or caught up in the trivialities of day to day existence at a sub-cerebral level that we are not even realizing that the ground is shifting away right under our feet. We are not realizing how COVID has affected the two pillars of Christian life, namely loving God with all our heart mind and soul and loving our neighbors like the way we love ourselves. We cannot shake hands, we cannot hug, we cannot stand near and talk, and we are losing meaningful human connections at every level to the extent that we are becoming like virtual images from a dystopian movie. We cannot go to church, take the eucharist or go to confession physically; and therefore, we have to satisfy ourselves with the moving images of priests and eucharists from distant places via the medium of YouTube. We are losing palpable connections. Grandparents in nursing homes cannot come near children or grandchildren, schools are not open, public gatherings are disappearing, places of worship are slowly disappearing, and "Brick and mortar" businesses are replaced by virtual giants like Amazon. Recently, this feeling was aptly expressed on the Twitter account of an Italian business professor named Gianpiero Petriglieri. He was expressing the angst of videocalls and zoom meeting as follows, "**It is easier being in each other's presence, or in each other's absence, than in the constant presence of each other's absence.**"

Think about it. It is futuristic and dystopian to think that people could be present and absent at the same time, but that is what is happening in the virtual world. The images of people are constantly there, but they are not palpable people. It is like a phantom, a mirage, or an illusion. Illusions bring neurosis, and COVID has brought a ton of them.

BEGOTTEN, NOT MADE

I always wondered what it means when someone says that a person is begotten or made. This is particularly important in Theology. I recently read an excellent explanation about the true meanings of these two terminologies in a book named "Mere Christianity" written by CS Lewis. Lewis was no small man. He fought in the trenches of World War I, and later became a Fellow in English Literature at Oxford University. He was elected to the Chair of Medieval and Renaissance Literature at Cambridge University. CS Lewis wrote that a man can only beget a man and not an animal. Similarly, a certain species of animal can only beget an infant of the same species. On the other hand, a man can make a statue or a tool. The statue or the tool is created and not begotten, because the statue or the tool is not a human being. We create something other than us, but we beget something essentially like us. We say about Jesus that He was eternally begotten of the Father, and not made. Jesus proceeds from the Eternal Father. Thus, the Father begets Him, and therefore He is consubstantial with the Father and therefore God. Jesus is begotten of the Father, and not made. What is begotten of God is God. What is begotten of man is man. We, the humans, on the other hand were made by the Father, and therefore we are not gods but humans. St. Joseph was created by God, and therefore he was a mere human being. Jesus was never created as He is God Himself. Jesus is the Creator. Jesus, who has no beginning or end, lives outside the confines of time. He lives in timelessness. Jesus, the alpha and the omega, the one who lives in all eternity without beginning or end, ruptured the space-time fabric and came to exist in time for thirty-three years for our sake.

Jesus, the Creator, subjected to Joseph, a created being, and called him Father. It needs radical humility for God to humble Himself to the level of His creature. It is revolutionary abasement on the part of God to become a human infant and depend entirely on two human beings (Joseph and Mary) for sustenance.

FAITH AND SNOW MAN

People have described the transformation from atheism to Christian faith using different symbols and images. CS Lewis described it as losing all defenses and melting like a snow man before the glory of God. It is akin to losing self-dependence and embracing total dependence on God. He described his feeling before conversion as if he were in a corset or suit of armor. When the conversion occurred, he felt as if he was a man of snow, melting drip-by-drip and trickle-by-trickle. It is a profound and interesting analogy. Mother Angelica, who founded the EWTN network once said, "Faith is one foot on the ground, one foot in the air, and a queasy feeling in the stomach." Clearly it is not easy to walk in faith alone. We do not see, but we still believe and trust the word of God. We become vulnerable like a melting snow man before the glorious light of God. It is a tough walk. Many will laugh at you or scorn. Some others may think that you are living in a fantasy world beyond the realms of reason and logic. Still others may believe that you are psychotic to trust an unknown God who challenges you to walk into unchartered territories.

The question is this: Why should any rational man enter this self-flagellation mode of life without perceiving any safety or security? Why should he walk with an "imaginary being" in faith?

The answer is simple. You will reach a stage where the call of truth is as strong as the call of the sea. The call is undeniable, irresistible, and full of surprises. It is the ultimate adventure, and the life of St. Joseph is the classic example of someone walking in faith. Joseph dreamt and then he obeyed the instructions received in the dream without questioning. He did not know the challenges before him when he ventured to go to Egypt, but still trusted God and immigrated to this unknown pagan land with his young wife and infant. He simply trusted God.

FEET IN MOTION

I did not know much about St. Joseph when I lived in Kerala, India. There was no incentive or tugging to know him then, because life was easygoing. However, I moved to a different State in India to study medicine, and for the first time I felt the anxieties of a sojourner. It has persisted since then. Somehow, I always felt like an outsider, and the constant feeling was that of a lost prince in a foreign land. Faith has helped me during my migration from India through UK to United States. I have worked as a physician in many hospitals across many cities in India, UK and USA, and there was always this sense of alienation. It was the feeling of being "lost in translation." The nagging pain of constant displacement led me to Joseph. Joseph himself was an alien in many cities, and his life was one of constant migration. He went to Bethlehem with his pregnant wife. He fled Israel to save Jesus. Egypt, the pagan superpower, sustained Joseph, Mary, and Jesus for many years. He escaped to Nazareth to avoid trouble. It was empathy that led me to Joseph, because an immigrant knows the heart of another immigrant.

St. Joseph is the patron saint of immigrants because he knows the heart of displaced people.

WEDNESDAY IS A GOOD DAY

Brimfield is a small town near Peoria, Illinois, with a population of 868 people. In 2019, I had the opportunity to confess, adore and attend mass on Wednesday evenings at the St. Joseph Church in Brimfield. Unfortunately, it is not happening in 2020 thanks to the coronavirus pandemic. I wondered why confession, adoration, and mass were held specifically on Wednesday evenings in this church named after St. Joseph. Recently I read that the church honors St. Joseph on Wednesdays. By tradition, Wednesday is the day of St. Joseph.

Saturday, particularly first Saturday of the month, is dedicated to the Immaculate heart of Mary. Friday, specifically first Friday of the month, is dedicated to the Sacred Heart of Jesus. Sunday is the Lord' day.

Wednesday is St. Joseph's day, and March is the St. Joseph's month.

DECEMBER 8,1870

December 8 is the Solemnity of the Immaculate Conception. However, the church had a double portion blessing on December 8, 1870. In addition to the day of the Immaculate Conception, it also became the historic day when Pope Pius IX declared St. Joseph as the patron of the Universal Church.

Joseph is the foster father of Jesus. He is also the father and patron of the Church which is the mystical body of Christ. It is said that the pope received more than five hundred letters from many Consecrated Religious requesting the declaration of St. Joseph's patronage of the Church. However, the pope was moved by a Dominican priest named Fr. Jean-Joseph Lataste who offered his life as a sacrifice and endured many mortifications to enable the declaration of St. Joseph as the patron of the church. Fr. Lataste died at the age of 36 in 1869, and the

99

Pope declared St. Joseph as the patron of the Church the next year.

ST FRANCIS XAVIER COLLEGE CHURCH AND THE SCULPTURE DEPICTING THE DEATH OF ST. JOSEPH

I vaguely remember my catholic relatives invoking the name of St. Joseph when older members of the family were in sick bed. They used to pray "Jesus, Mary, and Joseph-Have mercy on this poor soul." I forgot all about it until 2007 when I encountered a beautiful sculpture depicting the death of St. Joseph in St. Xavier's college church at St. Louis University. My daughter joined the university that year, and I have attended mass in that beautiful gothic church many times. I saw the beautiful sculpture of St. Joseph flanked by Virgin Mary and Jesus on either side. Mary was holing his hand, and Jesus was pointing to the heaven. It was sculpted by Joseph Sibbel in Renaissance and Baroque style using imported Carrara marble from Italy. Joseph had a happy death because he was in the safe hands of the Son of God and the mother of God. Can anyone ask for a better death? No wonder the Church invokes St. Joseph for a happy death.

JOSEPH AND THE LILY

One wonders why St. Joseph is often depicted as carrying a lily. In Christian symbolism, the white lily represents purity. Joseph was pure of heart. Lily also represents virginity and chastity, and Catholics call Joseph the most chaste husband of Mary.

Throughout catholic history, Joseph and Mary were considered the defenders and protectors of Virgins. Some authors like Cyril Robert has called St. Joseph the "Guardian of God's Lilies."

THE SEVEN JOYS OF A SHIPWRECK

How could there be joy in a shipwreck? But that is what happened to two Franciscan friars who suffered a shipwreck. They suffered a horrible shipwreck and held on to a plank to sustain life. They kept themselves alive for three days clinging on to the plank and praying to St. Joseph. On the third day the fury of the storm abated, the sky became clear, and a celestial being gently guided them to the shore. On reaching the shore, the two friars fell at the feet of the being supposing him to be an angel, but the celestial visitor told them that he was St. Joseph. Moreover, St. Joseph instructed them to say one Our Father and seven Hail Mary in honor of the seven joys of St Joseph. The church honors St. Joseph by reciting the seven sorrows and seven joys of St. Joseph. (Saint Joseph, as Seen by Mystics and Historians, Dr. Rosalie A. Turton, The 101 Foundation, NJ)

CAST OFF FROM THE NEST, SEPARATED FROM THE HERD.

Today is the feast of Our Lady of Sorrows. I was reading a Malayalam essay "Koodu Vittavar, Koottam

Thettiyavar(cast off from the nest and shunned by the herd) earlier today. It made me think about truth seekers in history who were treated as scum by their own people. Socrates was accused of impiety and was condemned to death. The prophets of Israel were terribly persecuted for telling the truth. The members of the Holy Family were glued to each other by love, but life was not easy for them. Theirs was a life of constant displacement. Joseph and his pregnant wife had to go in haste to Bethlehem to fulfil the decree of Caesar. Then came the flight to Egypt. After living in the land of Egypt, Joseph moved back to Nazareth. Jesus was denounced by the people of Nazareth, and again by the Jews in Jerusalem. After the crucifixion of Jesus, Virgin Mary moved to Ephesus with St. John the Evangelist. Early Christians were shunned by the Jews and the gentiles alike. Those who embraced the Way of the Nazarene were persecuted and marginalized by their family and friends. All the apostles except John the evangelist was martyred.

One must pay a heavy prize for telling the truth. Every truth seeker was ostracized by his community. It was true for Socrates, Jesus Christ, John the Baptist, and Joan of Arc. It is still true in communist countries and even in sophisticated democratic nations. The truth seekers are cast off from their nests and shunned by the herd. It is a type of martyrdom.

JOSEPH AND THE CHURCH

It took about 1400 years for the Church to officially honor Joseph, and the first official act of the Church in this regard was in instituting a feast of St. Joseph in 1479. Pope Sixtus IV instituted the feast. In 1726, the name of Joseph was inserted in the Litany of Saints. Pope Pius IX entrusted the Roman Catholic Church to the patronage of St. Joseph on December 8,1870. The Litany of St. Joseph was approved by Pope Pius X in 1909. Pope Benedict XV inserted the name of St. Joseph in the Divine Praises in 1921. Realizing the rise of communism, Pope Pius XII declared May 1 as the day of St. Joseph the worker. (Source: Saint Joseph as Seen by Mystics and Historians, Dr. Rosalie A. Thurton, 101 Foundation, Asbury, NJ, 2000)

St Joseph came late, but clearly with the rise of the Reformation, the French Revolution and Communism, the Church realized the power of St. Joseph. The last 500 years can be called the "Age of Saint Joseph."

THE UNBROKEN SILENCE OF JOSEPH AND THE DICTATORSHIP OF NOISE

Joseph is the saint of silence and internal life. He does not utter a single word. We do not hear him speak to Jesus or Mary. Matthew, Mark, Luke, and John have not penned a single letter or word that escaped from his mouth. None of the apostles, historians, or church fathers have ever recorded a single spoken word of saint Joseph. That brings us back to the question of the mystery and power of silence. The book of Wisdom says, "While gentle silence enveloped all things, and night in its swift course was half gone, your all-powerful word leaped from heaven, from the royal throne" (wis 18:14-15).

Liturgical tradition says that this verse is a prefiguration of the incarnation of the Word in the silence of the night at Bethlehem. Cardinal Sarah in his book, The Power of silence, talks about the dictatorship of noise. Cardinal Sarah argues "without silence, God disappears in the noise. Unless the world rediscovers silence, it is lost. The earth then rushes into nothingness." The Cardinal testifies that God abides in eternal silence, and only the man who drapes himself in silence can understand the manifestation of God. St. Joseph knew this, and in the silence of the day God communicated with him.

Modern man lives in a jungle of obscene images and disconnected noises. These images and noises are choking our conscience and killing our innocence. Every modern gadget is designed to impart a dictatorship of noise and shadows. We have lost our will for internal formation and recollection and are rushing into the abyss of darkness at an accelerating pace. We need to redeem ourselves by practicing silence and solitude by following the footsteps of Saint Joseph.

SANTO ANELLO, THE WEDDING RING OF JOSEPH?

A pious tradition in Italy honors a quartz ring believed to be the wedding ring of Joseph and Mary. This cult is called Santo Anello. The ring is kept in a reliquary at a chapel called Capella del Santo Anello. Many miracles are attributed to this relic, and traditionally pilgrims going to Assisi stop at this chapel to venerate the ring. It is a favorite among newlyweds for obvious reasons. Irrespective of the authenticity of this relic, the practice of this cult is useful to call to mind the dignity and holiness of the sacrament of matrimony.

THE SEVEN SORROWS AND SEVEN JOYS OF ST. JOSEPH

The Church honors St. Joseph by meditating on his seven sorrows and joys. The seven sorrows are as follows: St. Joseph resolving to leave Mary quietly, The poverty of Jesus' birth, The circumcision of Jesus, The prophecy of Simeon, The flight into Egypt, The return from Egypt and the loss of the Child Jesus.

Saint Joseph is also honored through the constant meditation of his seven joys. His documented seven joys are as follows: Annunciation of St. Joseph, The birth of the Savior, The Holy name of Jesus, The effects of the redemption, The overthrow of the idols of Egypt, Life with Jesus and Mary at Nazareth, and the finding of Child Jesus in the temple.

The Church encourages a Seven Sunday devotion to the joys and sorrows of St. Joseph.

(Source: Consecration to St. Joseph-The Wonders of Our Spiritual Father, Fr. Donald Calloway, Marian Press, Stockbridge, MA)

APPARITION OF ST. JOSEPH AT KNOCK

Few apparitions of Joseph have been recorded, and the one observed by more than twenty people occurred at Knock in Ireland in 1879. The apparition was like a tableau, and the characters in the apparition were all silent throughout the vision. There was Mary, the mother of God, in the center. St. Joseph and St. John the Evangelist appeared on either side of the Madonna. There was an altar by their side and a lamb and a cross could be seen on the altar. It was like the tableau of a paschal mystery.

St Joseph was seen with his head bowed respectfully towards Mary. Apparently, his skin was brownish, and his beard was grey. Joseph, Mary, and John did not speak a word. It looked as if they were contemplating on the Paschal mystery of the mass. A century later, Saint John Paul II came to Knock to honor Mary and Joseph, and by then the church had already accepted the apparition informally.

JOSEPH, THE ANTIDOTE FOR POSTMODERN TOXICITY

The postmodern world is unmoored from truth and is celebrating lies of every kind. It canonizes liars and persecutes the truth-seekers. Everyone is confused, and no one is exempt from this torrential downpour of unimaginable immorality. We eat for the sake of eating, and then worry about our weight. This leads to vigorous physical activity, calorie-counting, organic food, and food fads of all kinds. People overeat from lack of discipline, and practices gluttony as a privilege. Gluttony is a sin. We must contain it through moderation and temperance. Sex is the most lucrative and profitable business in the world, and the men and women in this business make billions by selling the bodies of vulnerable souls created in the image of God. St. John Paul II teaches us in his Theology of the Body that sex was created by God for spousal self-giving, procreation, and fruitfulness. Instead, man is diving deep into the abyss of lust. The antidote for lust is chastity. Wealth seems to be the ultimate yardstick of success, and people are selling their souls to capture wealth. Frugality and simple living are the anti-toxin for this sickness. Violence and anger are glorified. An attitude of gratitude is the remedy for this illness. Apathy and existential angst must be replaced by a joyful spirit. Pride and vain glory are the foundational sins of the day. Humility antagonizes pride.

St Joseph practiced temperance, fortitude, chastity, poverty, obedience, gratitude and humility. We should follow his footsteps to avoid the post-modern snares mentioned above.

A RIGHTEOUS FATHER

The gospel of Matthew describes Joseph as a "righteous man." It is sometimes easy and comprehensible to use real life examples of righteousness, rather than trying to define righteousness in abstract terms. What comes to my mind when I think of St. Joseph is the image of my father. My father was a righteous man. Many years ago, two well qualified young men from the parish applied for a teaching position in the parochial school. It came before the parish committee. One man was related to my father and the other was not. When it came to the committee, everyone voted in favor of my father's relative, but my dad voted in favor of the other man. As a unanimous decision could not be reached, the case was referred to the Bishop. The Bishop called my father and said, "Why did you vote against your own relative? Moreover, it was your family that donated the land for the church and the school, and it is only fair that someone from your family gets the teaching position in the school." My father replied, "Let me put two case scenarios before you. Both men are equally qualified. One is related to me and the other is not. My relative is qualified and rich. He has enough money to live without this job. He can get a job in any school with his qualification. The other man is dirt poor, and his parents and 5 siblings live a hand to mouth existence. If you put both cases on God's scale of charity, which way do you think the balance would tilt?" The Bishop was speechless, and later he confirmed the poor man as the new teacher. Our relatives did not forgive my father for letting down his own kin. Years later, the poor man and his siblings became very successful and for no reason they started a character assassination spree against my father. I know it hurt my father deeply. Twenty years later, my older brother asked my father, "Dad, if you could go back in time, knowing that the poor man would malign and hurt your name, would you still vote for him?" My father replied "Yes." I call this righteousness. Righteous people do the right thing even when it is unpopular. Men without guise stand up for the truth even when it hurts. Righteousness is not cheap. It is very costly.

MEN ARE LEADERS

God ordained men to be leaders of the family, and it is well-evident by observing the life of St. Joseph. Men have four roles to play as leaders. Time to time, politics change, and men must take up **political leadership** to protect family and society. Joseph was born into a society that had reached rock bottom in political morality. Herod was a murderous, lustful, and effeminate man who was subservient to the Romans for political gains. The Romans oppressed the Jews and taxed them heavily. The Jewish priests and the elites were absolute hypocrites. St. Joseph knew all this, and he protected his family from the prevailing political culture by fleeing to Egypt. The second leadership role is an **economic leadership**. From time immemorial, men have been providers to their family, and Joseph was no exemption to this rule. He worked as a carpenter and fed his wife and son. Men must assume **moral leadership** by teaching right and wrong and standing up for the truth. Joseph was a paragon in that respect. Eventually men also should assume **military leadership** to ward off physical and spiritual threats to the family. Joseph protected God and his mother, and he did that job very well.

As gender-bending theories are spreading like wildfire, men seem to have lost their calling and responsibilities to family and society by shying away from the God-ordained leadership roles.

SLEEPING ADAM AND BEAUTIFUL EVE. SLEEPING JOSEPH AND IMMACULATE MARY

The Book of Genesis describes how God caused Adam to fall into a deep sleep, and while Adam slept God created Eve from the man's rib. Adam and Eve disobeyed God and fell from grace. All of us inherited the fruit of their disobedience. Centuries later, St Joseph fell into a deep sleep. The book of Matthew says that when Joseph woke up from his sleep, he took Mary as his wife. Unlike our first parents, Joseph and Mary obeyed God and submitted to Him, and therefore God redeemed the entire human race through Jesus, their beloved Son. The Church Fathers describe another sleep. When Jesus was in his sleep of death on the cross, the centurion pierced his heart. From the side of Jesus, blood and water issued, and the church, the spouse of Jesus, was born on that day.

We can see the typology of spousal relationship in all these three situations. The first spousal relationship was flawed, the second marriage was perfect, and the third relationship was akin to a "mystical marriage."

YOUNG ADULTS LIVING WITH PARENTS

Young adults in USA do not live with parents. Thy move out. However, the rising student debt, unemployment, and the recent pandemic has forced many young adults to live with their parents. Many of these young adults feel desperate for living with their parents. They do not have to feel despondent, as they have a great ally in Jesus. Jesus, the Son of God, lived with his parents as a young adult! He did not feel inferior or less manly for living with Joseph and Mary. He moved out only when he was thirty years old. This should give hope for lot of youngsters living with their parents.

LUCIA, JOSEPH, AND FATIMA

Today is October 13, 2020. On this same day in 1917, people witnessed the Miracle of the Sun at Fatima, Portugal. Following the miracle, the Holy Family was seen standing next to the sun. Sr Lucia has recorded in her memoirs that St Joseph was holding Child Jesus. She saw St. Joseph and Child Jesus blessing the world. It was the final act of the final apparition at Fatima. It therefore must be symbolic and prophetic of the events to come.

Years later, Sr Lucia wrote, "There will come a time when the decisive confrontation between the Kingdom of God and Satan will take place over marriage and the family."

(Source-The Fight of Faith, That Man is You, Paradisus Dei). We are seeing Sr Lucia's chilling message unfolding before our eyes in 2020. One must be physically, mentally, and spiritually blind to deny the existence of this diabolical attack on families. Unbridled feminism, gender bending theories, perverse lifestyles, skyrocketing divorce rates, juvenile delinquencies, deliberate self-harm and substance abuse, riots, attacks on conventional family values, widespread acceptance of occultism, unhinged

111

abortion and even late-term feticide are accepted as norms in modern societies.

Today, we need Jesus, Mary, and Joseph more than anyone else.

THE DEATH RATTLE OF WESTERN CIVILIZATION

Intentionally or unintentionally, the current culture of globalism is eliminating and killing the Western civilization. Classic Western Civilization is based on Greco-Roman thinking and Judeo-Christian ethics. In a recent book called The Parasitic Mind, author Gad Saad lays down the principal parasitic thoughts that kills common sense. He classifies these parasitic thoughts into 8 categories and claims that these trends are largely responsible for killing Western Civilization by a thousand cuts. He identifies radical feminism, moral relativism, echo chambers devoid of intellectual diversity, postmodernism, culture of victimhood, identity politics, social constructivism, and political correctness as the main culprits responsible for the death and decay of Western Christian thought. Sadly, in my opinion, parasitic tentacles are choking Catholic thought to the extent that catholic laymen are unable to trust the secular and politically motivated decrees coming from secularized hierarchy.

Where do you find truth? It is imperative to return to common sense, family values, classic thoughts, and Judeo-Christian ethics or else, each one of us will turn into a zombie puppet in the hands of oligarchs and technocrats.

GALLONS OF INK, MILES OF CELLULOID, AND MILLIONS OF SOULS

When I came to USA in 2004, I accidently listened to a program called "Focus on the Family" aired by Dr. James Dobson. I listened to his talks on family values from 2004-2006, and I must confess that Dr. Dobson had an indelible impact on my thinking. Dr. Dobson believes that family is the bedrock of human civilization and any attack on family will jeopardize the entire framework of society. He incessantly fought against pornography, abortion, embryonic stem cell research, and perverse sexual relationship, for decades. Some people even consider him to be the single most important influence on shaping the thoughts on family values in evangelical America. He warned us about the scourge of pornography more than three decades ago and declared that we could win a "war on pornography." President Regan recommended him to the Attorney General's Commission on pornography. Gallons of ink have been spilled by promotors of obscenity to write ticklish stories that destroy manhood and families. Movies and TV shows with miles and miles of celluloid images have imprinted wrong imaginations in the minds of young people for generations.

St. Joseph should be the model of manhood, or else we will lose all anchors that hold families to a solid rock.

THE BLOSSOMING ROD OF JESSE

Every Christian is aware of the Old Testament prophecy, "There shall come forth a rod out of the root of Jesse, and a flower shall rise up out of his root." It is a sign about the Messiah and His family of origin. It was well known to the ancient Israelites that their Savior must come from the family of Jesse and David. The prophecy alludes to the genealogy of Jesus. St. Joseph is a direct descendent of King David, and tradition says that his rod blossomed to indicate that he was selected to become the spouse of virgin Mary. Every icon and statue of Joseph depict him with a budding staff. It looks as if the above prophecy is both symbolic and literal. Symbolic, because Jesus was born into the lineage of Jesse and David. Literal, because of the literal budding of Joseph's rod. Icons and pictures show white lily flowers blossoming from the tip of Joseph's staff. In Hebrew lily is Shoshana, and it represents purity. My daughter's middle name is Susan, and it comes from the Hebrew word Shoshana.

Down the centuries, Iconographers have used white lily to represent Virginal purity.

TENSION IN MARRIAGE-THE SILENCE OF MARY AND THE MEDITATIONS OF JOSEPH

Do not think that there were no tensions in the married life of Mary and Joseph. There was strain in the marriage at the outset itself. Angel Gabriel appears to Mary and tells her that she would carry the Son of God in her womb. Joseph was not made aware of this in the beginning, and therefore when he learns about the pregnancy, he becomes flabbergasted. Mary was not allowed to share the message of the angel, and therefore despite seeing the torments of her husband she remained mute. Joseph on the other hand does not want to embarrass Mary. Joseph is meditating and praying. He wants to know the will of God. He maintains restraint and equanimity in his behavior to Mary, and that itself is a source of pain for Mary. They went through this suffering for some time. Eventually, the angel comes to Joseph and tells him that Mary was conceived of the Holy Spirit. At this moment Joseph understands the gravity of the mission ahead of him. God has entrusted His Son to him. Joseph has become the custodian of Mary, the ark of the covenant.

This story proves that waiting, meditating, and praying are good tools in the hands of healthy couples.

GUARDIAN OF THE REDEEMER (REDEMPTORIS CUSTOS)

Saint John Paul II realized the unique graces that cascaded to the church through the heavenly conduit of St. Joseph. An apostolic exhortation in honor of St. Joseph was published on August 15,1989. It was named Redemptoris Custos. In that exhortation the Pope elaborated St. Joseph's role and ministry in details. Specifically, Joseph was named the Guardian of the Mystery of God. In few short sentences, the angel of the Lord revealed the mystery of God to St. Joseph. The angel said "Joseph, son of David, do not be afraid to take Mary as your wife, for the Child conceived in her is from the Holy Spirit. She will bear a son, and you are to name him Jesus, for he will save his people from their sins. In these sentences, there is the mystery of the Trinity, the mystery of Mary, virgin and mother, the mystery of the incarnation, and the mystery of the redemption of humanity from sins. The pope talks about Joseph the husband of Mary, and his attribute as a "just man." Furthermore, the dignity of labor and work as an expression of love is elaborated. The papal exhortation dwells into the interior life of the saint. The Pope also acknowledges St. Joseph's unique role as the patron of the church.

UNFAILING AND UNQUESTIONING FAITH

The church calls Abraham the father of faith. However, if we read the bible, we see that Abraham doubted his calling. He, under the influence of his wife Sarah, took Hagar as his wife, and had a child. Almost every prophet or patriarch asked for a sign from the heaven when a specific task was assigned to them. Gideon asked for a sign to believe what was told to him. Zachariah refused to believe the angel when he was told that his wife would conceive a son.

However, St Joseph always showed unfailing unquestioning faith. He never questioned or expressed doubt when he received messages from heaven. He obeyed the instructions immediately. He received difficult instructions usually in the middle of the night, but he carried it out then and there.

It is difficult for a modern man to comprehend the actions of St. Joseph. We are cautious, questioning, and doubtful when we make decisions based on "inspirations," and that is the right thing to do, as mystical experiences and inspirations can come from heaven or hell. However, Joseph was in constant communion with God, and he could easily discern messages coming from heaven.

THE SECRET LIFE OF JOSEPH

Joseph had an interior life unparalleled in history. He was in constant prayer. I remember seeing the Latin adage "Ora et labora" outside the St. Benedict's Abbey at Montecasino, Italy. It literally means "pray and work." St. Joseph's life was nothing but prayer and work. He had the unique privilege of leading a "double life", whereby he could remain in silent rapture while giving full exterior attention to the work in hand at his workshop. He enjoyed inner silence, rapturous joy, and constant communion with God. His soul was plunged in inexpressible delight while engaged in work. Physical fatigue or mental anguish could not drown the burning charity he experienced for the Creator and creature. He was experiencing the superabundance of heavenly joy, even when he was toiling in the fields. He found peace amid hunger, rejection, isolation, and pain. He could endure difficulties because of his strong inner life.

TEMPLE IN JERUSALEM, TEMPLE AT NAZARETH

A temple is a place where God is worshipped. The great temple of Jerusalem was the epicenter of Jewish religion, and animal sacrifices were offered there as per the law of

Moses. The Holy Family went to Jerusalem to celebrate the feast days. Though the Holy Family went to worship in Jerusalem to satisfy the law of Moses, their house at Nazareth itself was a temple. We know that the Ark of the Covenant was missing in the Temple at the time of Jesus, but Mary, the living Ark of the Covenant, lived in the humble abode at Nazareth. Jews offered animal sacrifices in Jerusalem, but the Lamb of God who came to take away our sins lived in Nazareth. The Old Temple in Jerusalem was fading away, and the Living Temple of Jesus was slowly encompassing the humanity. In the fullness of time the temple of Jerusalem was razed to the grounds by the Romans. Jesus is the Temple. Jesus is the Lamb of God sacrificed for our sins. Jesus is also the Eternal High Priest.

"PERSECUTION ABOVE GROUND AND PRAYER BELOW GROUND"

Persecution of Christians is on the ascendency everywhere, including the West. One must be prepared to face it in the years to come. I opened a book called Jesus Freaks, to see the lives of martyrs over the centuries. I bought this book in 2003 from a bookstall in Walsall, England. The book talks about the first Roman persecution under Nero, and it depicts the persecution of early Christians at the Roman Coliseum. Christians prayed in the catacombs. The book used the adage "persecution above ground and prayer below ground" to illustrate this point. We know about martyrs who have shed blood, but there are also martyrs who suffered mentally and physically without being killed. St. Joseph was such a martyr.

St Joseph through his suffering, fatigue, insecurities, and hard labor endured a slow martyrdom. Doctors of the church, theologians, saints, and mystics are of the opinion that St. Joseph also suffered white martyrdom as he knew about the impending passion, humiliation, crucifixion, and death of Jesus. He carried this pain throughout his life. Therefore, it can be said that Joseph suffered with the Redeemer and for the Redeemer.

JOSEPH, JESUS AND CARPENTRY

Little boys imitate their fathers. It is therefore obvious that the earliest memories of Jesus about his father might have centered around carpentry and the tools of carpentry. Joseph might have guided Boy Jesus to use the tools of carpentry in his shop. The Son of God, who created the universe, the angelic hosts, the billions of galaxies, and all types of creatures humbled himself to be taught by the hands of St. Joseph. He like his father was a carpenter by trade. Carpenters in Joseph's time made farm equipment like yoke and plough. No wonder Jesus used the imagery of farm tools in his parables. He told his disciples that his yoke is light. He taught them that anyone who wanted to enter the Kingdom of God should not look back. To illustrate this teaching, he told that the farmer who places his hand on the plough does not look back.

THE AMBASSADOR TO THE BOSOM OF ABRAHAM

The Jewish thought of afterlife at the time of Jesus is best reflected in the parable of Lazarus and the Rich Man. It was believed that the righteous souls went to a place of bliss and security called the "Bosom of Abraham." The wicked souls went to Gehenna, a place of perpetual torments. All the just men who died before the arrival of Christ went to the blissful abode of the dead named "Bosom of Abraham," and they all waited in limbo for the arrival of the Messiah. It is believed that when Joseph died, he went to the Bosom of Abraham, and announced to all the prophets, patriarchs, and just men that his son Jesus would come soon to carry them to a higher state of bliss.

Even today, Joseph is therefore considered the patron of happy death (Catechism of the Catholic Church, Second Edition, Libreria Editrice Vaticana, page 264)

NOT FOR ZEBEDEE BROTHERS, BUT FOR JOSEPH AND MARY

There is an interesting anecdote in the Bible. One day, the mother of James and John (Zebedee brothers) approached Jesus and asked him a favor. She wanted her sons to sit on either side of the throne of Jesus. Jesus replied that the two seats were reserved for those to whom the Eternal Father had destined to give. Theologians have always wondered who would be sitting on either side of Jesus. In the book The Life and Glories of St. Joseph, by Edward Healy Thompson and published in London and New York by Burns and Oates limited in 1891, he argues that St Joseph and Virgin Mary are sitting on either side of the throne of Jesus in heaven. It makes sense. Jesus still calls Mary mother, and Joseph father. It has not changed even though he is in heaven. Therefore, Edward Healy Thompson's argument seems valid. Fr. Donald Calloway, in his recent book, Consecration to St. Joseph: The Wonders of Our Spiritual Father believes that Mary, the mother of Jesus, sits on Jesus's right side, and St. Joseph, his father sits on the left side.

Joseph is preeminent among all saints, as he is the foster father of Jesus. He is sitting next to Jesus, and his intercessions are efficacious.

TWO MEN, TWO WOMEN, TWO DREAMS

Today, the word "love" is often used and misused by people and popular media. It happens because of our subjective and sensual interpretation of truth and love. It is not uncommon for men and women to lose the "flame and chemistry" in marriage and seek thrills in new "relationships." However, God is the absolute and objective standard of truth and love, and his laws have not changed down the centuries. He is the same yesterday, today and tomorrow. This could be illustrated by the examples of two men, two women, and two dreams down the centuries. The men are Abimelech and St. Joseph. The women are Sarah and Virgin Mary. When Abraham lived in Gerar with his wife Sarah, King Abimelech of Gerar, entertained active adulterous thoughts about Sarah. God persecuted Abimelech in his dream and said, "You are about to die because of the woman, She is a married woman." Abimelech repented, and God spared his life. Joseph was a just man, betrothed to his wife Mary. Joseph was afraid when he learned that Mary was pregnant. God speaks to him tenderly in his dream and told him not to be afraid to take Mary as his wife, as she was conceived of the Holy Spirit.

God honors sacramental marriage. He abhors adultery. It is all or none with God, and there is no middle ground.

JOSEPH AND HIS COAT OF MANY COLORS

The ancient Joseph had a coat of many colors. His father Jacob gave the special coat of many colors to his dearest son. In a similar way, God the Father has given a garment of many colors representing the many offices of St. Joseph

St Thomas Aquinas wrote "Some saints are privileged to extend to us their patronage with particular efficacy in certain needs, but not in others; but our holy patron St. Joseph has the power to assist us in all cases, in every necessity, in every undertaking." Thomas Aquinas lived during a tumultuous time in Europe, and his writings have perennial value. In 1231, the ban on Aristotle was lifted in Paris. Thomas studied at the University of Naples, and subsequently became a student at Paris under Albert the Great. He saw St. Louis initiating the Crusades. He was ordained a priest in 1251 and became Master of Theology in 1256. He died on the way to the Council of Lyons, and even though centuries have passed since his death, Thomas Aquinas's word is still considered the last word in Theology. It looks as if St. Joseph, like Joseph the Patriarch, is wearing a coat of many colors as he holds many offices and patronages in the opinion of Thomas Aquinas. We can seek St. Joseph's patronage in every situation unlike other saints who have specific offices. The church recognizes the patronage of Joseph in all the following areas:

1. Model disciples
2. Patron of the Church
3. Patron of Husbands
4. Patron of Fathers
5. Patron of family life
6. Protector of the unborn and pregnant mothers
7. Model of workers
8. Patron of emigrants
9. Model of humility and hidden life
10. Model of contemplative union with Christ
11. Patron of apostles
12. Patron of happy death (Source: *Saint Joseph as Seen by Mystics and Historians, Dr. Rosalie A. Thurton, 101 Foundation, Inc, Asbury, NJ, USA*)

TERESA AND ST. JOSEPH

The modern devotion to St. Joseph received an impetus during the lifetime of St. Teresa of Avila. Teresa was fully devoted to St. Joseph, and in 1621 she chose St. Joseph as the patron of the Reformed Order of the Carmelites. She got permission to celebrate the feast of St. Joseph on the third Sunday after Easter. This feast spread to other parts of the Spanish Kingdom. She, like St Thomas Aquinas, believed that St. Joseph was unlike other saints, since he could intercede to his Son for almost anything. She even challenged people to ask St. Joseph for favors and experience his goodness first-hand for themselves. There are many miracles attributed to St. Joseph during her lifetime. It is said that Teresa placed 12 of the 17 monasteries that she founded during her lifetime under the patronage of St. Joseph. (The Holy Family Devotion-A Brief History, Chorpenning, Joseph. F, St Joseph Oratory, Montreal, 1997)

EARTHLY FATHER AND ETERNAL FATHER

Jesus is the Son of God. He is the alpha and the omega. He is the Word Incarnate. He is the Second Person of the Trinity who took body from the Virgin Mary. He thus became the Son of Man. When the Son of God became the Son of Man, he needed a man in flesh and blood to assume the responsibility of fatherhood. God, the Eternal Father, from all eternity had reserved the privilege of fatherhood to St. Joseph. In other words, St. Joseph was given the huge responsibility to act on behalf of God the Father in taking care of Infant Jesus. Think about it – St. Joseph was conferred the privilege of fatherhood, by God the Father himself. It is a great office, and therefore, the mystical body of Christ has the right and responsibility to honor St. Joseph as their father.

HEAVENLY SPOUSE AND EARTHLY SPOUSE

St. Joseph is intimately linked to all three Persons of the Holy Trinity. We saw how Joseph is linked to God the Father. How is Joseph intimately connected to the Holy Spirit? Virgin Mary conceived of the Holy Spirit, and therefore the Holy Spirit is the eternal Spouse of Virgin Mary. St. Maximilian Kolbe goes as far as calling Virgin Mary "the created Immaculate Conception" and the Holy Spirit the "Uncreated Immaculate Conception." (Source-33 Days to Morning Glory, Michael E Gaitley, Marian Press). Mary and the Holy Spirit are inseparably attached. However, the Holy Spirit ennobles St. Joseph by giving him the privilege of becoming the earthly spouse of Virgin Mary. Joseph was assigned the role of protecting Mary and Infant Jesus. If Holy Spirit entrusted his Spouse to Joseph, how much more we must submit our lives to St. Joseph?

SAVIOR, SINS, AND SAVIOR OF THE SAVIOR

There are so many "churches" and "denominations" today that people have lost count of them. The self-proclaimed protestant pastors (Not the real pastors who preach on sins, salvation, and the old rugged cross) who proclaims the gospel of material wealth and positive thinking are proliferating like wild mushrooms in the woods. These people use Christ and the gospel to amass personal wealth and private jets. They do not preach the glory of the cross or the nature of sin. Jesus, the Son of God, came to earth for one purpose and for one purpose only: to save his people from sins. While proclaiming to Joseph that Mary had conceived Jesus; the angel mentioned to him that Jesus would save people from their sins. Joseph clearly knew that Jesus would not displace the Romans and assume an earthly kingdom. Joseph was aware of the future passion of Jesus. Joseph did not anticipate a militaristic, dictatorial Messiah who provided his people with money, power, or vanity. In fact, Infant Jesus was so vulnerable that Joseph had to assume the role of the "savior of the savior." Joseph endured his sufferings well, as he was in tune with the will of God. He was realistic and wise because he always searched the truth.

"THY FATHER AND I HAVE SOUGHT THEE SORROWING"

Jesus, Mary, and Joseph attended the great feasts in Jerusalem. It was a happy time. Members of the family, friends, and extended family walked from Nazareth to Jerusalem to participate in the Jewish celebrations every year. After returning from Jerusalem, Joseph and Mary who were travelling separately in the company of men and women, found to their dismay that Jesus was missing. They were extremely scared, sad, and guilty. They rushed back to Jerusalem, and on the third day found Jesus debating with the elders in the temple. It was three days of extreme passion and sorrow for Mary and Joseph. In fact, it was a foretaste of the things to come. Mary tells Jesus that his father was very sorrowful (Note - Mary does not say "foster father," suggesting the preeminence of Joseph in the life of the Holy Family).

Mary gave uttermost respect to Joseph, and Jesus called him "father."

JOSEPH'S 90-MILE WALK IN THE DEPTH OF WINTER

The Advent season of 2020 Christmas has just started. Christmas lights and trees are out, but unlike other Christmas times, people are quite anxious this year thanks to the COVID-19 pandemic. It is nice to identify with the anxieties of Joseph and Mary, who celebrated the first Christmas in a real manger. Joseph and Mary had to travel 90 miles from Nazareth to Bethlehem, first over the flatlands of Jordan river, and then over the hilly terrains around Jerusalem. Many bandits and outlaws roamed the desert, and wild animals like boars and bears attacked travelers. It was wintertime and temperatures reached freezing points in the night. In addition, Mary was fully pregnant, and therefore they could not have travelled more than 10-20 miles a day. They also had to carry water, dried bread, and fruits to sustain life during this perilous journey. Joseph could not find an Inn, and Mary gave birth to the Son of God in a cave full of animals. Hopefully, this could give some encouragement to us in times like this.

NO ROOM IN THE INN

What if Joseph and Mary were searching for an Inn or restaurant during the 2020 COVID/advent season? This was the thought that was coming to my mind when I read the passage in the bible about Joseph not finding a room in the Inn. It would have been extremely stressful to Joseph and Mary to see how they were wandering around in Bethlehem looking for a place to stay. Every inn refused admittance to them. Eventually they found refuge in a cave where animals dwelt. Joseph never complained to God. He probably never understood why the Eternal Father allowed his Son to be born in a cave full of animals. The ways of God are mysterious to men. Jesus taught about the final judgement later in his life. He differentiated the sheep and the goat, the righteous and the wicked, based on their actions. The righteous let foreigners and strangers in, while the wicked chases them away. It is obvious that there were some wicked men in Bethlehem who refused admittance to Joseph and Mary in their house.

FORTY HOUR EUCHARISTIC ADORATION. THIRTY YEAR EUCHARISTIC ADORATION

It is a common practice to adore Jesus in the Eucharist. One such pious practice is the 40-hour Eucharistic adoration. We believe that Jesus is truly present as body, blood, soul, and divinity in the Holy Eucharist. However,

St. Joseph adored the body, blood, soul, and divinity of Jesus for 30 years. What a privilege!

It is believed that Joseph died before Jesus started his public ministry. Therefore, St Joseph must have adored Jesus for at least 30 years. Joseph had the privilege to carry Jesus, protect and clothe him, and even teach him the law and the art of carpentry.

ST. JOSEPH, THE GUARDIAN OF GOD'S LILIES

There is a book on St Joseph written by Cyril Robert and published by the Marist brothers in 1945. It calls Joseph the guardian of God's lilies. Who are God's lilies? In Christian symbolism, lily represents the following:

1. Purity
2. Virginity
3. Resurrection
4. Humility

Virgin Mary is the prime example of virginity, purity, and humility. However, down the ages, countless saints lived chaste and pure life. Many of them like Maria Goretti were martyred for their purity and chastity. Lily also represents resurrection and that is why we have Easter lilies. Lily of the Valley represents humility. When the breeze blows, the lilies of the valley bow down in humility. St Joseph is the guardian of saintly men and women who practice humility and chastity.

MARRIAGE AND THE VOW OF CHASTITY

It is a paradoxical to state that a couple who had taken the vow of chastity were joined in marriage. The catholic theology, particularly St. John Paul's Theology of the Body, explicitly states the importance of mutual self-giving and fruitfulness in marriage. The body of the female belongs to the man and vice versa.

Virgin Mary took a vow of Virginity and St. Joseph also vowed to remain chaste. God brought them together in Holy Matrimony. However, their union was spiritual in nature. They brought up Jesus, the source of all fruitfulness. It was a unique marriage.

THE FIRST CENTURY JEWISH HOME

Jesus, Mary, and Joseph must have lived just like any Jew of the first century. The son always followed the footsteps of the father, and it was imperative that the father taught the son about the techniques of his profession. People sat on the mud floor, cross legged, and ate their meal. They did not use forks or knives. Women wore a head veil and men wore turbans. Men wore long shirts stretching to the ankles. Women drew water from the village well, kept the fire burning, and did all the cooking. Women did the weaving at home. Men woke up early and went to work in the farms before sunrise and usually returned home at dusk. They ploughed the fields and reared their sheep and goats. They ate lamb, fish, legumes, and bread. Figs and grapes were the favorite fruits. Three times a year they went to Jerusalem to participate in the great feasts of the Jews.

FEASTS OF PASSOVER, PENTECOST AND TABERNACLES

The ancient Jews celebrated Passover, Pentecost, and the feast of Tabernacles. Almost all men went to Jerusalem to participate in these feasts. So, by argument Joseph must have gone every year to Jerusalem except when he was in Egypt. Children and women usually accompanied men, particularly for the Passover festival during Springtime. Pentecost was the first-fruits festival, and it also commemorated the Jews receiving the Torah from Moses. The festival of the Tabernacles coincided with harvest, and Israelites remembered their 40-year desert-wandering during that festival.

We know the incident when Jesus was lost and found during one of those festivals. It is safe to assume that Boy Jesus had gone multiple times to Jerusalem with his parents to participate in these great feasts.

BOY JESUS AND SHEMA YISRAEL

In the Second temple period, people of the Jewish diaspora faced Jerusalem and prayed "Hear, O Israel: the Lord our God, the Lord is one." Every Jewish father taught his son to pray the Shema Yisrael. It was prayed in the morning and evening, and children were encouraged to pray this before going to bed. It was an affirmation of the monotheistic nature of the Jewish God, and his exclusive covenant with the Jewish people. St. Joseph must have taught Jesus to pray Shema Yisrael facing the temple in Jerusalem while living in Egypt and Nazareth. Jews resisted falling into the trap of polytheism while living amid gentiles by repeatedly reciting the Shema.

MARY IN THE OUTER COURT, JOSEPH IN THE INNER COURT

Mary is the biological mother of Jesus. Joseph is the foster father of Jesus. However, the Jewish law did not permit women in the inner courts of the Temple. Joseph alone was permitted in the inner courts. Joseph and Mary took Baby Jesus to the Temple, as per the requirements of the Jewish law. It was supposed to be for the purification of the mother, and the offering up of the firstborn. Joseph and Mary took turtle doves for oblation. It was at this time that Simeon the righteous and Anna the prophetess blessed the Child and his parents.

Mary submitted to Joseph despite her exalted position. Mary followed the law, though she was the mother of God.

THE SUN ALSO RISES, BUT IN THE EAST

Hemingway wrote the famous novel Sun Also Rises. The devotion to St. Joseph remained dormant in the Western Hemisphere for almost a millennium. However, devotion to St. Joseph was practiced in the eastern hemisphere ever since the beginning of Christianity. The sun rose first in the east and it took a millennium for the rays of

St. Joseph's devotion to reach the West. The Coptic church in Alexandria, the Syrian Church of the east, and the Greek Orthodox church honored Joseph for centuries. Gradually, the influence of the monks and the religious from the east influenced the Latin Christians of the West. The interactions between the East and the West during the great Councils led to the interchange of ideas. The crusaders received first-hand knowledge of eastern Christianity during the many battles they fought in Palestine and Egypt. Joseph remains hidden in the gospels. Likewise, he remained hidden in Christendom for centuries.

MASSACRE OF INNOCENTS AND THE TEARS OF RACHEL

It is Christmas Season, and people are reminded of the story of the three wisemen, king Herod, and the massacre of the innocents. We all know the story. The three wisemen see the star and come in search of the newborn king. Kings are born in palaces, and therefore the wisemen go to the palace of Herod in search of the baby prince. Scholars look through ancient documents and inform Herod that the Messiah is prophesied to be born in Bethlehem. Herod tells the wisemen to let him know the whereabouts of the newborn. The wisemen find Baby Jesus but are warned by the angels to avoid Herod. Herod gets angry and kills all infants below two years of age. There was much weeping in Bethlehem. The Bible allegorically calls it the weeping of Rachel. Joseph is warned in a dream to flee to Egypt. Joseph thereby saves the life of Jesus.

Innocents are massacred today. The euphemism for that massacre is abortion and prochoice. Rachel is still weeping.

ST. JOSEPH AND THE CANADIANS

The history of Canada is very much linked to devotion to St. Joseph. Iroquois Indians attacked Fort St. Ignatius, St. Louis and Sainte-Marie in mid-March 1630, and everyone had recourse to Saint Joseph, Patron of Canada. The Iroquois fled in panic on March 19th, the feat day of the saint. Canadians believed that St. Joseph saved them from the siege of Quebec in 1690. The departure of Bostonians in 1776 was also attributed to St. Joseph. In 1711 Admiral Walker moved towards Quebec with 88 vessels and 12,000 men. People prayed to Joseph and Mary. The Admiral had to turn back as ten vessels were wrecked, and a battle was avoided. St. Joseph is the patron saint of Canada, and he is also credited with the rapid abatement of the 1847 Typhoid epidemic in Ottawa (Source: Arrow Guide, Saint Joseph's Oratory, Montreal)

ST JOSEPH AND THE EVANGELICAL COUNSELS

The Evangelical Counsels of Poverty, Chastity, and Obedience are signs of the Kingdom of God. The Consecrated Religious among us have taken the vows of poverty, chastity and obedience. Poverty requires trust in divine providence, that God will provide for our needs. Jesus told his disciples not to take food, money or sack so that they could learn to rely on God. In obedience, we submit our will to the will of God like the way Jesus submitted himself to his Father in the garden of Gethsemane. In practicing chastity, we are reminded to restrain our bodily desires. It helps to raise our minds to noble thoughts and actions.

St Joseph is the classical example of a person who has perfected the Evangelical Counsels to the utmost. We therefore can seek his help when assaulted by impure thoughts, greed, and rebellion.

THE HOLY FAMILY AND THE DONKEY

In ancient Palestine, poor people probably owned a donkey. A donkey was useful for Joseph to go up the hills of Judea with the tools of his trade. When Joseph and Mary had to go from Nazareth to Bethlehem, Mary might have used the family donkey. It is inconceivable to think that Mary and Joseph carried the newborn baby and walked all the way to Egypt. They must have used their family donkey for this purpose. Donkey was a beast of burden, and often Christians are reminded to be beasts of burden for God and people.

PATRON OF THE UNBORN

Catholics uphold the dignity of human life from the moment of conception to natural death. Human soul is created in the image of God, and hence every human life has immense value. A fetus is not a blob of tissue, but an invaluable soul. Destruction of fetus in its mother's womb is nothing but the shedding of innocent blood. The Bible says that the blood of Abel is crying before God, and hence every drop of innocent blood cries to God for justice. Joseph protected the dignity of Mary when she was found pregnant. He knew the law of Moses and did not want to shame Mary. God reveled to Joseph that the baby in her womb was none other than the Incarnate God. Joseph saved the baby and his mother, and therefore he is still the patron of pregnant mothers and unborn children.

FULGENS CORONA

2020 will be remembered as the year of Corona. Hence any mention of Corona is attributed to this despised virus. However, Fulgens Corona (Radiant Crown) was an encyclical of Pope Pius XII. The encyclical was promulgated in 1954 to celebrate the centenary of the proclamation of the Immaculate Conception of Virgin Mary. Many theologians have wondered if St. Joseph was immaculately conceived or taken to heaven in body like Mary. St. Bernadine of Siena who had great devotion to St. Joseph had mentioned about these possibilities. However, the pope, in this encyclical, unequivocally declared "Mary obtained this most singular privilege, never granted to anyone else, because she was raised to the dignity of the mother of God."

Therefore, we know from the teachings of the Church that St. Joseph was born with the original sin like anyone of us. It does not diminish the virtue of St. Joseph, but in fact it increases his merits. He attained extraordinary levels of virtue and sanctity, even though he was born with the original sin. That makes him a hero.

NAZARETH, SYNAGOGUE, AND CARPENTRY

Jesus grew up in Nazareth. His father taught him the Shema and the skills needed to become a good carpenter. They went to the synagogue at Nazareth on the Sabbath day. Jesus would have had his education in the school next to the synagogue. Such schools were called the "House of the Book" as the book of the Law were taught there. Pupils seated on the ground level learned to read, write, and count by forming letters and numbers on the sand or pottery, and rarely on papyrus. The teacher recited a text out loud and the children repeated and repeated and repeated it until the lesson was firmly fixed in their memories (Source: The World of Saint Paul, Joseph M. Callewaert, Ignatius Press, San Francisco). Surely people in Nazareth must have known Jesus very well. Later when he returned to Nazareth as an adult, people were expectantly waiting to hear from him, and might have even wanted to see a miracle. He was therefore given the scroll of Isaiah. People were impressed by his teaching and some of them wondered "Isn't this Joseph's son?" However, things changed when Jesus compared Capernaum to Nazareth. People did not like to hear that Capernaum was better than Nazareth, and understanding their thoughts Jesus said, "No prophet is accepted in his hometown." It did not end well, and his own people drove him out of Nazareth. After his incident, Jesus mostly taught at the Synagogue in Capernaum.

THE DEMONS CALL HIM "JESUS OF NAZARETH."

Nazareth might have rejected Jesus, but demons still identify him as Jesus of Nazareth. There must have been a spiritual reason for Joseph to select Nazareth as the boyhood town of Jesus. The Gospel of Luke mentions the incident at the Synagogue in Capernaum. Jesus was teaching in the Synagogue and a man possessed by an evil spirit cried out, "What do you want with us, Jesus of Nazareth? Have you come to destroy us? I know who you are-the Holy One of God."

Thanks to Joseph, Jesus is still known as the Holy One of God from Nazareth.

ST. JOSEPH AND THE ANTIPHIONS OF ADVENT

St. Joseph was the last link that connected the Old Testament to the New Testament. He initiated the New Testament but did not live to see it unlike the Blessed Mother. Virgin Mary saw the mission of Jesus, his passion on the cross, his death, burial, resurrection, ascension to heaven, arrival of the Holy Spirit and the beginning of Christianity, but St. Joseph was not a witness to any of these events. Joseph, the venerable man, had no part in the public ministry of Jesus. His life, as always, was hidden. He lived the life of a devout Jew and died like one. However, he transferred the messianic promises of the prophets, the law, and the psalms to Boy Jesus, as can be seen from the Antiphons of the advent. These antiphons were composed in the seventh century by the monks, and it is full of Old Testament expectations of the messiah. Joseph, along with other pious Jews, were waiting for the fulfillment of the promises. Joseph saw the Incarnate Wisdom, Adonai, Root of Jesse, Key of David, The Dayspring, The King, and the Emmanuel fulfilling in its totality on the day Jesus was born. It is interesting to note that Jesus inherited the titles, Key of David and Root of Jesse, through his father Joseph who was a direct descendent of Jesse and David.

A NEW DEVOTION TO "SLEEPING JOSEPH"

I remember one of the professors in Medicine who taught me long time ago. One day she was talking about the Catholic devotion to Infant Jesus. She was amused at this "silly devotion." She was wondering why Catholics should develop a specific devotion to Infant Jesus when multiple devotions already exist for the adult Jesus. She added, "Catholics are very inventive in these areas." It was clearly a sarcastic statement.

I was not aware of a devotion to "Sleeping Joseph" until recently. I read this in an article about Pope Francis. Apparently, the Pope used to keep a statue of sleeping Joseph on his desk when he was a Cardinal in Argentina. He brought it to Vatican when he was elected Pope in

2013. He claimed that whenever he had a problem, he wrote it down on a small piece of paper and placed it underneath the statue of sleeping Joseph. He argued that Joseph would dream about the problem and come up with an answer. I have not tried this yet, but I am sure many people are practicing this devotion. I have seen "Sleeping Joseph" statues in many Catholic Shops.

JOSEPH'S LULLABY

Catholics have been honoring Joseph and Mary since the beginning of Christianity. Both names are mentioned in the mass, and there are umpteen number of devotions to them. Catholics do not pray to Joseph and Mary but ask them to intercede for us. However, Protestants do not think about Joseph or Mary at any time other than Christmas. They sing "Mary did you Know" and "Joseph's Lullaby" strictly during Christmas time. They remember Joseph and Mary along with the angels, wisemen, shepherds and the cattle. When Christmas is over, the figurines of Mary, Jesus, Joseph and the wisemen go back to its original place in the attic. Therefore, I was amused when I head "Joseph's lullaby" from a protestant radio yesterday. In the lullaby, Joseph is singing to Infant Jesus to avoid the weight of his glory and the prize he must pay for a moment, so that he can sleep like a baby in his hands.

JOSEPH AND THE RED DRAGON

The Book of Revelation, in its dramatic final chapters, reveals the cosmic battle between the Red Dragon and the people of God. No one exactly knows the mystery of the symbolism of the Red Dragon. However, some theologians have hypothesized the Red Dragon as a tyrannical communist antichurch fighting against the Church of God. In the late 19th and early 20th century, the Catholic church had to face the rapid rise of communism in European countries. The Church studied the false philosophy and economic agenda behind the communist movement. In order to combat the International Worker's Day (May Day) that lured Catholic workers into the communist camp, Pope Pius XII proclaimed May 1st of every year as the feast of St. Joseph the Worker.

St Joseph the worker labored in obedience to the law of God. He did this with equanimity, fortitude, and holy abandonment. He is the model of every worker.

BAR MITZVAH OR SON OF THE COMMANDMENT

The coming of age for boys in Jewish tradition is called the Bar Mitzvah. It became a religious ceremony among Jews in the medieval times and did not exist at the time of Jesus. However, a rudimentary form of such a practice must have existed as evidenced in the Gospel of Luke 2:41-47. In the event described by Luke; the 12-year old Jesus stayed back in the Temple at Jerusalem rather than accompanying his parents back to Nazareth. After 3-days of searching his parents found him debating with the scholars of the Law in the Temple. Mary asked him "Why have you treated us so? Your father and I have been looking for you anxiously." It is interesting to note his reply. Jesus replied "Did you not know that I must be in my Father's house?"

Was Jesus telling his parents that he had reached the age of reason, and that he was transitioning from boyhood to adulthood? Was he reminding them about his future passion, death, and resurrection? Was he also hinting that St. Joseph's role is slowly eclipsing and Eternal Father's role is beginning?

18 YEARS OF BIOGRAPHY CONDENSED IN A SENTENCE

After the Temple incident at the age of 12, Jesus returned to Nazareth. The rest of his private life from age 12 to 30 is condensed in one sentence by the gospel writer. The gospel of Luke says, "He went down with them and came to Nazareth and was obedient to them." Then he adds, "Jesus increased in wisdom and in years and in divine and human favor.'

In an age of rebellion, disobedience and juvenile delinquency; the power packed sentence that condenses the 18-year biography of Jesus must be food for thought for every boy and girl.

THE GOSPEL OF INFANT JESUS AND VIRGIN MARY

Luke's gospel talks about Virgin Mary and the infancy of Jesus more than other gospel writers. We do not know why, but probably Luke talked to the Blessed Mother herself before writing the gospel. It is unique in mentioning the annunciation and visitation in detail. Luke describes the shepherds adoring Infant Jesus, the Good Shepherd. He goes on to mention the purification ceremony. It was Luke who wrote about the 12-year old Jesus visiting Jerusalem with his parents. He gives more details about Boy Jesus staying back in the Temple to debate with the priests and the scribes. The Evangelist also depicts the anxiety of Joseph and Mary, and their eventual relief on finding Jesus in the temple. For all these reasons, the gospel of Luke may also be considered the gospel of Mary and infant Jesus.

REDEMPTORIS CUSTOS

In the above-mentioned apostolic exhortation, Saint Pope John Paul II calls Joseph the guardian of the mystery of God. He highlights St. Joseph's characteristic as a just man. The Pope further elaborates how work is an expression of love. The Holy Family grows through the silence of interior life. It is in this context that Jesus is said to have grown in "stature and wisdom." The Holy Family set the stage for this growth under the paternal leadership of St. Joseph. The Pope again entrusted the church to the patronage of St. Joseph. If Jesus needed Joseph to grow in stature and wisdom, how much more his mystical body (the Church) needs Joseph for its own growth?

LITANY OF ST. JOSEPH

The current Litany of St. Joseph was approved by Pope Pius X in 1909. The litany calls him the light of patriarchs, probably because he went to the Bosom of Abraham to enlighten the patriarchs about the impending arrival of Jesus, the Messiah. It also enlists the known attributes of St. Joseph. He was just, chaste, prudent, strong, obedient, and faithful. The foster father of Jesus embraced poverty, affliction, and sickness with equanimity. The Pope calls him the pillar of families and the glory of home life for obvious reasons.

The Pope's original name was Giuseppe (meaning Joseph in Italian). The pope was clearly honoring his patron saint.

SACRED HEART OF JESUS, IMMACULATE HEART OF MARY, AND THE LOVING HEART OF JOSEPH

When I was growing up in India, our house had the portraits of the Sacred Heart of Jesus and the Immaculate Heart of Mary portrayed prominently in the front porch of the house. It was a tradition among Catholics to honor the loving hearts of Mary and Jesus in the house. I also remember the priest imparting a solemn blessing of the Sacred Heart of Jesus on our family after installing the picture of the Sacred Heart of Jesus. It was the year 1968, and I was an elementary school pupil in our parochial school. I had no clue what it meant, but over the years I figured out the significance of these devotions. These are well established devotions in the Catholic world, irrespective of whether you are in Latin America, Africa or Asia.

Joseph is always late. He waits in silence. He gives way to his wife and Son and avoids the center stage.

However, who can deny the burning love of Joseph for Jesus, Mary, and the Church? His heart was on fire for Jesus. A lot of bad things happened in 2020, but God can bring blessings amid afflictions. 2020 will be remembered as the year of COVID-19. Colleges and schools were closed, and therefore I had the opportunity to dedicate my family to St. Joseph. It is worth noting that the formal devotion to the Holy Family was started by Saint Francois de Laval, the first bishop of Quebec, Canada.

THE OBELISK AND THE SOLAR CULT

The ancient Egyptians worshiped the Sun-god. They erected temples and obelisks in honor of the sun-god. One such city is Heliopolis, literally meaning "city of the sun." Many of these sun temples have disappeared, but ancient prophets like Isaiah, Jeremiah and Ezekiel had explicitly condemned the practice of sun-worship. Isaiah prophesied "the Lord rideth upon a swift cloud and shall come into Egypt. The idols of Egypt shall be moved at his presence, and the heart of Egypt shall melt in the midst of it." Many mystics and fathers of the Church attribute the arrival of Jesus in Egypt as the fulfillment of this prophesy. Some people even believe that idols fell from their pedestals when the Holy family moved in.

JOSEPH, THE "MAN OF THE HOUSE."

If Virgin Mary was the immaculate mother of God, and Jesus was conceived of the Holy Spirit, then what was the purpose of Joseph in that family? The answer is

145

simple-even when Virgin Mary was the mother of God, she was not a priest! Man is the priest of the family! Joseph was the priest of the Holy family! Like a priest, and the son of a true king, he defended Mary and Jesus. He was a true man.

A man is the priest of the family. He leads the family in spiritual matters and offers himself as a "Living sacrifice" on behalf of his wife and children. He makes tough decisions and work hard for the family. He defends his territory like a true king and protects the purity of his family. He preserves his home like a "hallowed ground" and protects his family from intruders.

Joseph is the true model of manhood. Mary submitted to his authority. Jesus obeyed him. The Holy Family is the model for every family.

THEY ALSO SERVE WHO STAND AND WAIT

I started writing about St. Joseph in 2014, after publishing my book A Tryst with Mary. When I told about my plan to one of my cousins, he replied "No one writes about St. Joseph, so I guess he will be happy to hear that you are writing about him." I did not like that statement, because I thought he was disrespectful to St. Joseph. After writing a few pages, I changed gear. For some inexplicable reason, I started writing my book The Battle Hymn of the Eucharist and published it in 2019. After its publication, I resumed writing about St. Joseph. Today is December 8, 2020. My wife told me that Pope Francis had just declared a yearlong celebration honoring St. Joseph to commemorate the 150th anniversary of St. Joseph being declared patron of the universal church. I was happy. What came to my mind was the famous lines from John Milton's poem. When Milton was becoming blind, he wrote, "They also serve who stand and wait." St. Joseph stood and waited on his Son and wife. He patiently waited for centuries before the church honored him. He gave way to the Tryst with Mary and the Battle Hymn of the Eucharist, before he allowed me to write about him. He is the epitome of radical humility.

I AM A NAZRANI

I am a St. Thomas Roman Catholic Syrian Christian from Kerala, India. For generations our forefathers were called Nazranis. Nazrani is an Arabic term for Christians, and it was derived from the Aramaic word Nasraya. It could also be Anglicized as "Nazarene," meaning the followers of Jesus of Nazareth. Jesus was strongly associated with the town where he grew up that even his followers were called by the name of that town. It is not an accident that Joseph built his house in Nazareth. It was the will of God that Jesus would be known as the Nazarene.

St. Thomas, the apostle, was the only apostle to preach outside the Roman empire. He travelled through the Middle East to Persia, and from there to Southern India sailing across the Arabian sea. He converted our forefathers to the "Way" of Christ, and was martyred in Chennai, India. Our Church had hierarchical relationship with the church of Persia, and this led to the adoption of East Syriac (Suriyani, a dialect of Aramaic) liturgy in Kerala. Westerners called us Syrian Christians as we worshipped in Suriyani, and Hindus and Muslims in Kerala called us Nazranis.

LAK MAR YAWSEP (YOU, ST. JOSEPH)

I was listening to a CD of Syriac chants from Kerala, India. The CD is called Qambel Maran. It was released by Joseph J Palackal who has a doctorate in ethnomusicology from New York. One chant caught my attention. It was a Syriac hymn in praise of St. Joseph called Lak Mar Yawsep. The CD has many hymns in Syriac, and some of them were originally composed by St Ephrem himself. However, Lak Mar Yawsep was unique in many aspects. It was relatively new to the St. Thomas Syrian church, as it was composed in the 17th century. Unlike many other hymns, this hymn was composed by a Westerner who studied Syriac. An Italian Jesuit priest named Joseph Beschi (1680-1747), popularized devotion to St. Joseph among the Syrian Christians of Kerala by composing this chant. The chant was sung in praise of St. Joseph during the Novena prior to the feast of St. Joseph (March 19th). Joseph Beschi died in Kerala in 1747. (Source: Qambel Maran, Syriac Chants from South India, Joseph J Palackal, 2002)

Devotion to St. Joseph arrived late in the Syrian Catholic church of Kerala, India. As always, Joseph waits.

POSTCONCILIAR ICONOCLASM AND THE ECLIPSE OF ST. JOSEPH

I remember Our Lady of Lourdes church, Neericad, India. It was my boyhood parish. In the mid-sixties, our church had a statue of St. Joseph with infant Jesus. I used to gaze at that statue, and even imagined that St. Joseph looked like a pious old man from our village. The old man was affectionately called Kutty Chettan. He was a pious gentleman who wore a large scapular, and every time I saw him, I thought of St. Joseph. Statues remind us about transcendental beauty, and sometimes it quickens our devotions. However, the theological intellectuals of the mid-twentieth century thought otherwise. They hated gothic cathedrals, ancient chants, Syriac, Latin, and even statues of saints. The post conciliar madness secularized the church and led to a new form of iconoclasm. Many statues were removed from the pedestals and dumped in the attic. Our church also had a taste of the iconoclasm that was unleashed after the Vatican ecumenical council of 1962-65. St. Joseph was unceremoniously kicked out of the church. I had a chance to visit the church in early 2020, and the statue of St. Joseph is still missing. I wondered, "Is this progress or regression?"

THE MIRACULOUS DNA STAIRCASE OF SANTA FE

A few years ago, my wife received a YouTube video on the miraculous staircase of St. Joseph, from a friend of hers. The stairway is located at the Loretto chapel at Santa Fe, New Mexico. It was a true marvel of craftmanship, and many legends are attributed to its origin; and so, we decided to see it. We couldn't get a straight flight from Chicago, and we therefore flew to Los Angeles and took the connecting flight to Santa Fe. We reached the airport

149

past midnight, rented a car from the airport, and drove to the hotel. We reached the hotel at 2 AM. The next day we visited the Loretto chapel and saw the miraculous staircase. We stayed there for a few days and saw the Basilica, Fiesta, art museums, cross of the martyrs and other local attractions.

The Loretto chapel was built in 1873, by the Sisters of Loretto. The choir loft was built without stairs as it would have used much floor space. The sisters found it difficult to use a ladder to climb the choir loft, and so they did a 9-day novena to St. Joseph, the patron saint of carpenters. On the ninth day, an old gray-haired, gray-bearded man arrived there, leading a donkey. He had few basic tools like a saw, a carpenter square and a hammer. He worked on a staircase for few months and disappeared with out taking any payment from the sisters. The stairway confounds architects, engineers and master craftsmen to this day. It is built like a DNA double helix and takes two complete 360-degree turns and stands 20-feet tall without any central support. It rests solely on its base and against the choir loft. It is literally a floating staircase. It has 33 steps, corresponding to the 33 years Jesus spent on earth. It was made of a previously unknown wood species, and it was assembled using wooden pegs without any trace of glue or nails. Engineers have come up with three hypotheses but has not reached a consensus, and many experts admit that the physics of this staircase is beyond comprehension. The scientists are still scratching their heads for a viable explanation, but the nuns already have their answer. They believe that St. Joseph himself built the staircase. (Source: Loretto Chapel, The Miraculous staircase. M.M.K Brokaw, The Creative company, R.L. Ruehrwein, Publisher, Lawrenceburg, IN, 2011)

The stairway is still called the miraculous staircase of St. Joseph

THE DYING JESUS IS FROM NAZARETH, THE RISEN JESUS IS FROM NAZARETH, THE ASCENDING JESUS IS FROM NAZARETH

What ever is the current state of the town of Nazareth; one cannot forget that Nazareth is still known in time and etched in eternity as the inseparable "surname" of Jesus. When Jesus was crucified, Pontius Pilate wrote above his head "Jesus, the **Nazarene**, King of the Jews." It was written in Hebrew, Latin and Greek. The Jews objected, but Pilate was adamant. He said, "What I have written, I have written." It was risky for Pilate to write that Jesus was the King of Jews as it amounted to a rebellion against the absolute kingship of Roman Caesar. He still took the risk and wrote it on the cross. The King of the Jews is wearing a crown of thorns. His throne is the wood of the cross. He came from the despised town of Nazareth, and therefore was a **Nazarene**. (Remember what Nathanael said, "Can anything good come from Nazareth?)

Later Saul persecuted the early Christians in Jerusalem and was on his way to Damascus to persecute more Christians. Suddenly a light from heaven flashed around him, and he fell on the ground. He heard a voice saying to him, "Saul, Saul, why do you persecute me?" He asked, "Who are you, Lord?" The reply came, "I am Jesus, the **Nazarene**, whom you are persecuting." It can be clearly seen that the glorified body of Jesus is also known as Jesus, the **Nazarene**. Glorified Jesus cannot be persecuted, and therefore the persecution of every Christian is a persecution of the **Nazarene**.

Nathanael and many other elites despised Nazareth. However, the second person of the Holy Trinity wants to be known by the name of his father's town.

JOSEPH, THE PATRON OF EXILES

I am from India, a land where each State speaks a different language. I did my undergraduate and post graduate medical degrees in a State that spoke a different language. I taught in a Medical School in that same State. I emigrated to Great Britain in 1996 and worked as a Physician there until 2003. I moved to USA in 2003 and have been studying and working in this country since then. I understand the challenges of an immigrant cut off from family, friends, and native tongue, while living in a foreign land. I therefore can empathize with St. Joseph. Joseph also must have suffered poverty, isolation, inability to visit the Temple in Jerusalem and many other privations of exile. Joseph therefore is called the patron of the exiles. He can therefore empathize with all immigrants irrespective of cast, creed, or culture. It is a universal emotion shared by every immigrant, and Joseph epitomizes each of those emotions.

IF I AM A FATHER, WHERE IS THE HONOR DUE ME?

In the book of Malachi, God the Father speaks to his people through the prophet. He asks, "A son honors his father, and servant their master. If then I am a father, where is the honor due me?" It echoes down the centuries. Jesus is the utmost and the ultimate. He is the paragon of obedience. He obeyed his Heavenly Father every step of the way. He submitted to his foster father Joseph in extreme humility. If Jesus, the Son of God, obeyed and respected St. Joseph, then what is holding us back from honoring St. Joseph? Is it arrogance, intellectual pride, false theology, or inferiority complex? Whatever the case may be, the result is nothing but indifference to the affairs of St. Joseph. We need to wake up from this slumber and recognize this saint of saints, this father of all fathers, and this great light of patriarchs. God can unleash food from the granaries of Joseph during these times of spiritual drought and starvation. Joseph, the Patriarch, oversaw the granaries of Pharaoh. St. Joseph oversees the granaries of God.

THE PERPETUAL VIRGINITY OF MARY AND THE CHASTITY OF JOSEPH

St. Luke describes the annunciation as follows, "The Holy Spirit will come upon you, and the power of the Most High **will overshadow you**; therefore the Holy One to be born shall be called **the Son of God.**" By this statement, the angel is declaring to Mary that God would enter into a marital relationship with her causing her to conceive His Son in her womb. In ancient Israel the euphemisms for marriage were, "to lay one's power (Reshuth) over a woman," and "to overshadow by spreading the cloak (Tallith)," and these exact words are used by the angel in this encounter. The oral law of Kiddushin states, "The husband prohibits his wife to the whole world like an object which is dedicated to the sanctuary." (Kiddushin 2b, Babylonian Talmud). When Joseph was enlightened in the dream that Mary was bearing the Son of God, he must have remembered the Kiddushin that prohibited Mary to anyone other than God. Joseph knew that God had conducted Himself as a husband in regard to Mary. She was now prohibited to him for all time, and for the sake of the Child and Mary he could only live with her in an absolutely chaste relationship (Source: Born of the Ever Virgin Mary, Brother Dr. Anthony M. Opisso, Association of Hebrew Catholics, 4120 west Pine Blvd, St Louis, MO. 1995.)

THE CANADIAN CONFERENCE ON DEMENTIA AND THE HEART OF BROTHER ANDRE

In late October 2011, I attended the Canadian Conference on Dementia, at Montreal in Quebec. Once the conference was over, I visited the world's most important sanctuary of St. Joseph. The Saint Joseph Oratory was built in 1904 by Brother Andre. Brother Andre Bessette was considered beatified as per the 1982 decree of St. John Paul II, and declared a Saint by Pope Benedict in 2010. Andre Bessette was born in 1845. His father died when he was nine, and his mother three years later. Poor, sickly, and with little education, the young orphan found work in neighboring villages and later in the textile mills of New England. Later he joined the Congregation of Holy Cross as a brother and worked as a humble porter at Notre Dame college. He had great devotion to Saint Joseph, and people attributed many cures through his intercession. He attributed all the miracles to St. Joseph and built a chapel for St. Joseph in 1904. The little chapel grew to become the present Saint Joseph Oratory. This huge Basilica constructed in the Italian renaissance style holds the tomb of Saint Andre (Source: Arrow Guide, Saint Joseph Oratory, 3800, Queen Mary Road, Montreal, Canada). The heart of Saint Andre is still preserved separately as per the ancient custom prevalent among the French Catholics. When brother Andre died in January 1937, more than a million people came to pay tribute to him braving the winter snow of Montreal.

After visiting the tomb and the heart of the saint, I had an opportunity to confess my sins to a French priest. I remember the priest asking me to spell out my sins slowly in English as he had difficulty with fast paced English.

THE SCHOOL OF NAZARETH

Family is the basic unit of society, and the Holy Family sets the gold standard for family values. Fidelity, purity, charity, hope, and faith were practiced to perfection by the members of the Holy Family. The Holy Family is a miniature church (**Ecclesia Domestica)** and a prototype for all families (St

John Paul II, Redemptoris Custos). It is therefore important for every father and mother to imitate the virtues of Joseph and Mary. We know that family values are under diabolical attack, and probably that was the reason Jesus, Mary and Child Jesus appeared to the visionaries of Fatima on the last day of the apparition (October 13, 1917).

Catholic Churches are vanishing in many cities due to poor attendance, and 2020 has brought fresh challenges to congregations all over the world thanks to the Coronavirus pandemic. In these difficult times, the prophetic words of St. John Paul II regarding Ecclesia Domestica (Domestic church) becomes even more relevant to all believers.

PIUS X AND THE PIOUS UNION OF ST. JOSEPH

Saint Pius X encouraged a saint named Luigi to start an apostolate that would offer daily prayers for the suffering and dying. It is called the Pious Union of St. Joseph, and this association has its headquarters in Rome with branches all over the world. St. Luigi encouraged devotion to St. Joseph particularly among terminally ill patients. In the beginning of twentieth century, the theory of Darwinian evolution catapulted the concept of Eugenics. The Eugenic Evolutionists like Charles Darwin, Francis Galton, and Ernst Haeckel ushered in the era of "Mercy killing" (Source: The Architects of the Culture Of Death, Donald de Marco and Benjamin D Wiker, Ignatius Press), and realizing the danger of this scourge Pope Pius X and St. Luigi popularized devotion to St. Joseph among sick and elderly people. The Eugenic scourge was further popularized by Derek Humphry, Jack Kevorkian and Peter Singer, and the authors mentioned above described these men as Death Peddlers. It is important to emphasize the dignity of the human soul in every person, and particularly in the most vulnerable people living in Hospice care. The devotion to St. Joseph is a strong bulwark against the culture of death.

CORONA, PATRIS CORDE, AND CORONATION OF ST. JOSEPH

I wanted to meditate and write about St. Joseph for some time. However, it was in 2014 that I started penning my first few thoughts on St. Joseph. Later I changed my idea and started writing about the Eucharist. After completing my book on the Eucharist in 2019, I resumed writing about St. Joseph. I was therefore pleasantly surprised when I heard that the pope had declared 2021 as the year of St. Joseph. 2020 was a strange year, and I am happy that the year is ending in few days. The world has changed a lot since the onset of the 2020 COVID-19 epidemic. Social interactions, travel, and family reunions are scarce, and experts are inventing new words like "New Normal" and "Great Reset," to explain life in the post-pandemic world. I therefore feel it was appropriate for the Pope to initiate the coronation of St. Joseph during this coronavirus pandemic. The church has always instructed "Ite Ad Joseph" (Go to Joseph), as the way forward during difficult times. It is my hope that Joseph would guide us in the bleakest nights infested with fear and nightmares, and take us to Jesus, our eternal anchor. On December 8, 2020, the Pope declared a year long celebration of the fatherhood of Joseph. His apostolic letter, "Patris Corde" (with a father's heart), will certainly help us to rediscover the greatness of St. Joseph. Let us remember the fiat of Mary and Joseph and step out to the new world with courage.

A RHAPSODY FOR JOSEPH, THE QUINTESSENTIAL FATHER.

Caesar has come and gone. The statues of Alexander can be seen in the neglected corners of ancient museums. Napoleon is sleeping on the tattered pages of history books. Joseph, the simple carpenter from Judea, lives on as a beacon of hope in this post-COVID madness called "The New Normal." Beauty lies dormant, marinated with faith and hope, in the simple elegance of family life. That is the silent message of St. Joseph amidst the dictatorship of unhinged noise. I created this rhapsody on St. Joseph when my pen hit the papyrus over a 5-year period. It is my hope that this "Widow's Mite" may be a pleasing offering to St. Joseph in the cosmic coffers of endless time. With this thought in mind, I place my pen at the feet of St. Joseph in the year of Our Lord 2021 which the Vicar of Christ has declared as the year of St. Joseph.

ACKNOWLEDGMENTS

The following books helped me in my meditations on St. Joseph.

1. The Life and Glories of St. Joseph. Husband of Mary, Foster-Father of Jesus, and the Patron of the Universal Church. Grounded on the Dissertations of Canon Antonio Vitali, Father Jose Moreno, and other writers, By Edward Healy Thompson, MA. Second Edition. London and New York. Burns & Oates, Limited. M.H Gill& Son, Dublin, 1891. Library of the Union Theological Seminary, New York, Digitalized by Google.

2. Saint Joseph, As Seen by Mystics and Historians. Dr. Rosalie A. Turton, The 101 Foundation, Inc, P.O. Box 151, Asbury, NJ, USA.

3. Consecration to St. Joseph: The Wonders of Our Spiritual Father, Fr. Donald H. Calloway, Marian Fathers of the Immaculate Conception, Marian Press, Stockbridge, MA,01263, USA.